Sean McMahon was born in Derry in 1931. Educated at St. Columb's College, Derry, and Queen's University, Belfast, he now teaches mathematics and co-ordinates dramatic activities at St. Columb's College. He has edited and compiled several books, including *The Best of the Bell* (1978), and is author, with Risteard MacGabhann, of *Conradh na Gaeilge agus an tOideachas Aosach* (1981). He devotes his spare time to literary pursuits, regularly reviewing fiction for the *Irish Press,* contributing articles to magazines, and writing and performing in his own dramatic entertainments. Sean McMahon is married with four daughters and one son.

Eamonn P. McVey

10 June 1995.

Rich and Rare

A Book of Ireland

Sean McMahon

POOLBEG

First published 1984 by
Ward River Press Ltd

This edition published 1987 by
Poolbeg Press Ltd.,
Knocksedan House,
Forrest Great,
Swords, Co. Dublin, Ireland.

Selection © Sean McMahon,
1984, 1987

Reprinted July, 1994

ISBN 0 905169 86 7

Cover design by Steven Hope
Typeset by Cahill's Ltd., East Wall Road, Dublin 1.
Printed by The Guernsey Press Co. Ltd.,
Vale, Guernsey, Channel Islands.

For Mary Clare

ACKNOWLEDGEMENTS

Grateful thanks is due to the following for permission to reprint copyright material:

Mrs. Irene Calvert for "The Ballad of William Bloat" by Raymond Calvert; Mr. Simon Campbell for "The Gartan Mother's Lullaby", "My Lagan Love", "The Spanish Lady" from *Poems of Joseph Campbell;* The Dolmen Press for "The Planter's Daughter" from *Collected Poems* by Austin Clarke; Mrs. Maire O'Sullivan for "She moved through the Fair" by Padraic Colum; the author for "Ballad to a Traditional Refrain" by Maurice James Craig; Oxford University Press for "Pangur Ban" translated by Robin Flower from *The Irish Tradition;* Mr. Oliver D. Gogarty for "Golden Stockings" from *Collected Poems* by Oliver St. John Gogarty; the author and Blackstaff Press for "Ulster Names" from *Within Our Province* by John Hewitt; Mrs. Katherine Kavanagh for "A Christmas Childhood" and "Shancoduff" from *Collected Poems* by Patrick Kavanagh; Walton's Ltd. for "The Rose of Mooncoin" and "Biddy Mulligan" by Seamus Kavanagh and "Whack fol the Diddle" by Peadar Kearney; Faber and Faber Ltd. for "Dublin Made Me" from *The Hungry Grass* by Donagh MacDonagh; Ms. Margaret Marshall for "Me an' Me Da" by W.F. Marshall; Walton's Ltd. for "Three Lovely Lasses" by Delia Murphy; the Estate of the late Flann O'Brien and Granada Publishing Ltd. for "A Pint of Plain" from *At Swim-Two-Birds* by Flann O'Brien; Walton's Ltd. for "The Stone Outside Dan Murphy's Door" and "The Garden where the Praties Grow" by Johnny Patterson; the Executors of the Estate of Helen Waddell for "I Shall Not Go to Heaven" by Helen Waddell.

Poolbeg Press apologise for any errors or omissions in the above list and would be grateful to be notified of any corrections that should be incorporated in future editions of the book.

Contents

Introduction   15

I
Let Erin Remember

Lillibuléro   *Anonymous*   21
The Battle of the Boyne   *Anonymous*   24
Croppies Lie Down   *Anonymous*   27
The Wearing of the Green   *Anonymous*   29
Last Words   *Robert Emmet*   30
The Maiden City   *Charlotte Elizabeth*   33
The Burial of Sir John Moore   *Charles Wolfe*   35
The Ballad of Henry Joy   *Anonymous*   37
Bold Phelim Brady, Bard of Armagh   *Anonymous*   39
Dolly's Brae   *Anonymous*   41
Oh! The Praties They Are Small Over Here
   Anonymous   43
Old Skibbereen   *Anonymous*   44
The Shan Van Vocht   *Anonymous*   46
Tone is Coming Back Again   *Thomas Francis Mullan*   48
Dark Rosaleen   *James Clarence Mangan*   50
The West's Asleep   *Thomas Davis*   52
The Memory of the Dead   *John Kells Ingram*   54
O'Donnell Abu   *Michael Joseph McCann*   56
The Celts   *Thomas D'Arcy McGee*   58
The Boys of Wexford   *Robert Dwyer Joyce*   60
The Croppy Boy   *William McBurney*   62
The Rising of the Moon   *John K. Casey*   64
The Irish Colonel   *Sir Arthur Conan Doyle*   66
Boolavogue   *Patrick Joseph McCall*   67
Marching Song of Fiach MacHugh
   Patrick Joseph McCall   69
Rody McCorley   *Ethna Carbery*   71
Bold Robert Emmet   *Thomas Maguire*   73
The Men of the West   *William Rooney*   75

Panegyric at the Graveside of O'Donovan Rossa
    Patrick Pearse   77
The Man from God-Knows-Where
    Florence Wilson   80
Easter 1916: Proclamation of the Irish Republic   84
Solemn League and Covenant   86

II

The Ireland in the Heart

The Irish Dancer   *Anonymous*   89
Ireland Delineated   *Justice Luke Gernon*   90
I Am Raftery   *Anthony Raftery*   91
Protestant Boys   *Anonymous*   92
The Green Little Shamrock   *Andrew Cherry*   94
The Minstrel Boy   *Thomas Moore*   95
She Is Far From the Land   *Thomas Moore*   96
The Orange Lily-o   *Anonymous*   97
The Sash My Father Wore   *Anonymous*   98
Song for July 12th, 1843   *Jean de Jean Fraser*   99
A Nation Once Again   *Thomas Davis*   101
God Save Ireland   *T. D. Sullivan*   103
On Behalf of Some Irishmen Not Followers of
        Tradition   *George Russell (AE)*   105
I Am Ireland   *Patrick Pearse*   107
Renunciation   *Patrick Pearse*   108

III
The Pleasant Land of Erin

County Mayo *Anthony Raftery*	113
The Meeting of the Waters *Thomas Moore*	114
Biddy Mulligan: The Pride of the Coombe	
Seamus Kavanagh	115
Cockles and Mussels *Anonymous*	117
Dicey Reilly *Anonymous*	118
Waxies Dargle *Anonymous*	120
The Bells of Shandon *Francis Mahony*	122
Dawn on the Irish Coast *John Locke*	124
The Spanish Lady *Joseph Campbell*	127
On the Banks of My Own Lovely Lee	
Jonathan C. Hanrahan	129
Going Home *Patrick MacGill*	131
Galway *Mary Davenport O'Neill*	133
At Oranmore *Anonymous*	134
The Ould Lammas Fair *Anonymous*	136
I'll Tell My Ma *Anonymous*	137
Ulster Names *John Hewitt*	138
Dublin Made Me *Donagh MacDonagh*	140

IV
The Next Market Day

The Low-Backed Car   *Samuel Lover*   145
The Next Market Day   *Anonymous*   147
Four Ducks on a Pond   *William Allingham*   148
The Stone Outside Dan Murphy's Door
   Johnny Patterson   149
The Donovans   *Francis A. Fahy*   151
Danny   *John Millington Synge*   153
Riders to the Sea   *John Millington Synge*   155
The Wayfarer   *Patrick Pearse*   169
A Soft Day   *Winifred M. Letts*   170
Me an' Me Da   *W. F. Marshall*   171
Three Lovely Lasses in Bannion   *Delia Murphy*   174
Shancoduff   *Patrick Kavanagh*   176

V
The Wild Freshness of Morning
Evening's Best Light

I Saw from the Beach   *Thomas Moore*   179
The Last Rose of Summer   *Thomas Moore*   180
The Dying Girl   *Richard d'Alton Williams*   181
The Fairies (A Child's Song)   *William Allingham*   184
Bantry Bay   *James Lynam Molloy*   186
If I Was a Lady   *Percy French*   187
The Gartan Mother's Lullaby   *Joseph Campbell*   189
I Shall Not Go to Heaven   *Helen Waddell*   190
My Aunt Jane   *Anonymous*   191
A Christmas Childhood   *Patrick Kavanagh*   192
Wee Hughie   *Elizabeth Shane*   195

VI

I Know My Love

Cailín Deas Crúite na mBó (The Pretty Milkmaid)
Anonymous 199
The Enniskillen Dragoon   *Anonymous* 201
Kitty of Coleraine   *Charles Dawson Shanley/*
Edward Lysaght 203
I Know My Love   *Anonymous* 204
Kathleen Mavourneen   *Julia Crawford* 205
The Rose of Aranmore   *Anonymous* 206
My Mary of the Curling Hair   *Gerald Griffin* 207
The Spinning Wheel   *John Francis Waller* 209
The Lark in the Clear Air   *Samuel Ferguson* 211
Carrigdhoun (Lament of the Irish Maiden)
Denny Lane 212
The Rose of Tralee   *William Pembroke Mulchinock* 213
Slievenamon   *Charles J. Kickham* 214
I'll Sing Thee Songs of Araby   *W. G. Wills* 215
The Garden Where the Praties Grow
Johnny Patterson 216
Maire, My Girl   *John K. Casey* 218
Trottin' to the Fair   *A. P. Graves* 219
Gortnamona   *Percy French* 221
John-John   *Thomas MacDonagh* 222
Golden Stockings   *Oliver St. John Gogarty* 224
My Lagan Love   *Joseph Campbell* 225
She Moved Through the Fair   *Padraic Colum* 226
If I Was a Blackbird   *Anonymous* 227
The Planter's Daughter   *Austin Clarke* 228
The Rose of Mooncoin   *Seamus Kavanagh* 229

VII
Irish Humour, Wet and Dry

Aqua Vitae *Richard Stanihurst*		233
from A Modest Proposal *Jonathan Swift*		235
Johnny, I Hardly Knew Ye *Anonymous*		237
Stanzas on Women *Oliver Goldsmith*		240
The Friar of Orders Gray *John O'Keefe*		241
Let the Toast Pass *Richard Brinsley Sheridan*		242
Sir Boyle Roche *Sir Jonah Barrington*		244
The Finding of Moses *Zozimus*		247
The Agricultural Irish Girl *Anonymous*		249
Coortin' in the Kitchen *Anonymous*		250
The Cruiskeen Lawn *Anonymous*		252
I Don't Mind If I Do *Anonymous*		254
Let Him Go, Let Him Tarry *Anonymous*		256
The Maid of the Sweet Brown Knowe		
Anonymous		258
The Old Orange Flute *Anonymous*		260
There's Whiskey in the Jar *Anonymous*		262
Tim Finnigan's Wake *Anonymous*		264
The Women are Worse than the Men *Anonymous*		266
Father O'Flynn *A. P. Graves*		268
Phil the Fluther's Ball *Percy French*		270
Shlathery's Mounted Fut *Percy French*		272
The Curse *John Millington Synge*		274
The Liberator and Biddy Moriarty *Anonymous*		275
Whack Fol the Diddle *Peadar Kearney*		278
The Ballad of William Bloat *Raymond Calvert*		280
A Pint of Plain is Your Only Man		
Flann O'Brien		282
Ballad to a Traditional Refrain		
Maurice James Craig		283
Thompson in Tir-na-nOg *Gerald MacNamara*		284

VIII
The Trimmin's on the Rosary

St. Patrick's Breastplate *Anonymous*   309
Pangur Bán *Anonymous*   311
Columcille the Scribe *Anonymous*   313
While Shepherds Watched Their Flocks By Night
   Nahum Tate   314
Silent O Moyle *Thomas Moore*   316
All Things Bright and Beautiful
   Cecil Frances Alexander   317
"We are the music-makers"
   Arthur   319
O'Shaughnessy
Sheep and Lambs *Katherine Tynan*   320
The Trimmin's on the Rosary *John A. O'Brien*   322
To My Daughter Betty, The Gift of God
   Thomas Kettle   326
By the Short Cut to the Rosses *Nora Hopper*   327

IX
Sweet Inishfallen, Fare Thee Well

The Moon Behind the Hill *William Keneally*   331
The Irish Emigrant *Lady Dufferin*   333
O Bay of Dublin *Lady Dufferin*   335
Song from the Backwoods *T. D. Sullivan*   336
The Old Bog Road *Teresa Brayton*   338
Off to Philadelphia *Anonymous*   340
Come Back, Paddy Reilly *Percy French*   342
The Mountains of Mourne *Percy French*   344
The Emigrant's Letter *Percy French*   346
Corrymeela *Moira O'Neill*   348
Mary from Dungloe *Anonymous*   350

Biographical Index   353
Index of Titles   375

Rich and Rare

Thomas Moore

Rich and rare were the gems she wore,
And a bright gold ring on her wand she bore,
But oh! her beauty was far beyond,
Her sparkling gems or snow-white wand,
But oh! her beauty was far beyond,
Her sparkling gems or snow-white wand.

"Lady dost thou not fear to stray,
So lone and lovely thro' this bleak way?
Are Erin's sons so good or so cold,
As not to be tempted by woman or gold?
Are Erin's sons so good or so cold,
As not to be tempted by woman or gold?"

"Sir Knight! I feel not the least alarm,
No son of Erin will offer me harm;
For though they love woman and golden store
Sir Knight! they love honour and virtue more!
For though they love woman and golden store
Sir Knight! they love honour and virtue more!"

On she went and her maiden smile
In safety lighted her round the Green Isle;
And blest for ever is she who relied
Upon Erin's honour and Erin's pride.
And blest for ever is she who relied
Upon Erin's honour and Erin's pride.

Introduction

It is almost a sociological cliché that the Irish because of their history (and, I suspect, their temperament) are more susceptible to the oral in art than to the graphic. A dispossessed nobility and the peasantry they were forced to join had no scope for, nor indeed right to, the grander arts of theatre, painting or even the printed word. Drama, opera, ballet, ensemble music, painting, sculpture, the novel, the epic poem, all perforce urban arts, or at least the arts of a hierarchical society, played very little part in the lives of the people. Their art was folk-music and song, the ballad or the short tale. Three centuries of necessity hardened into instinct and even now, with universal literacy, the rapid urbanisation of the East and the growth of much greater aesthetic awareness throughout the country, there is still a native tendency towards the short piece, the solo item. The continuing success of the revised folk tradition, the proliferation of short story writers, the popularity of radio art, all suggest that in spite of television and the much greater availability of "Art" people still have an ear for and the patience for the quickly assimilable, easily recalled piece.

Irish lyric and narrative poetry, pieces of oratory, epigrams and proverbs and above all, songs—the easily carried treasure of a people either on the move or too bound to toil for greater leisure—are as popular now as when the weekly *Nation* began to bind together the fragmented people. There is a store, to use the Gaelic word for something precious, of this near-oral tradition which acts as a kind of inter-personal passport for all Irish people. It is not great art but beyond art, and for a majority of people who would disclaim all artistic interest it is a kind of culture that is alive, self-perpetuating and the possession of the Plain People of Ireland.

Rich and Rare is a selection, merely, from this treasure house. It is confined to material that was once in print: pieces remembered from schools or feiseanna, songs sung in pubs or round the fire or on the way home from football matches, poems that yield their meanings without agony, stirring recitations that used to sound in concerts in village halls, party pieces, the whole rich variety of what early critics used call the Common Muse.

The material chosen has been, for the sake of order (and for the reassurance of the compiler), arranged in categories. At once one must face the problem of borderline cases. The section on Irish history once contained material that created its own category, one that might have in a more innocent age been called patriotic, if that word had not become even more the last refuge of a scoundrel since Dr Johnson's day. Since the sixteenth century, Irish history, Orange and Green, has been a much more emotional affair than any decent theatre director would have permitted. As with Shelley, "Our sweetest songs are those which tell of saddest thought," and the ballads and poems about past events are seldom able to deal with victory. Gallantry, noble dying, sad recall of pitifully outnumbered defiance, the fading of new hopes: that enshrinement of old disappointments make up the material. The chance of the peace and the serenity to consider Ireland as a country or a mistress for whom it was not necessary to die was largely unavailable. The history category, "Let Erin Remember", with its "Boolavogue", "The Boys of Wexford", and "Croppies Lie Down", records in song and ballad the events, "The Ireland in the Heart" the love-story. "I am Ireland", "A Nation Once Again", "The Orange Lily-O" may not be very subtle expressions of feelings but their sincerity is clear.

With Ireland the green country, the topographical paradise, the ground is less of a minefield, except in what one dares to leave out. People have sung about Killarney and The Bells of Shandon who have never experienced the soft heavy air of those deep south places and it is probably true that every townland and parish from The Ould Lammas Fair to The Banks of Somebody's Lovely Lee has its own dedicatory poem or song. That 'tis but three miles from Derry to the Bridge at Drumahoe is a firm geographical fact as indisputable as that it is six miles from Bangor to Donaghadee. Ardee has its turfman, Buncrana its train and Mayo its moonlight but it would take a book as big as the Bog of Allen to contain all the local hymns that deserve inclusion. So in this as in those other sections, on Irish life in town and country, on Irish Humour, wet and dry, on Love (in which the Irish are marvellous theoreticians), there is so much material that severe selection had to be enforced.

The other categories—those dealing with Youth and Age, and such elusive ideas as Religion and Philosophy — are staple ingredients in all anthologies and our particular cave of treasures is full of much material both rich and rare. One section, the most Irish of all, sadly enough, deals inevitably with exile and the suspicion felt by many that Irish people only become fully fledged when they spread their wings at the last glimpse of Erin.

Any anthologist is a sitting target for the critic, lay and professional. In the case of *Rich and Rare*, incredulity, rage even, at wrong-headed exclusion (to say nothing of perverse inclusion) is perfectly proper. For every Irish man and woman has his or her own Rich and Rare against which this one may well clash and from which it will inevitably fall short. This particular selection attempts to be as widely applicable as possible. Not all the pieces are *particular* favourites of mine but in an absolute, if not in a comparative, sense each deserves its place. If my thumb-print appears more heavily than it should, I can only repeat that *all* choices are personal but after more than fifty years of Irish life I can claim to be as much in touch with the old sow or Cathleen Ni Houlihan as the next braggart and my offering is not gratuitously idiosyncratic. Besides I take some consolation from the fact that the pieces that readers most miss were certainly part of my original cull and did not survive the cuts.

I take this opportunity to thank Philip MacDermott of Ward River Press, whose idea this book originally was, his remarkable assistant, Margaret Daly, and my firm but gentle editor, Hilary O'Donoghue, without whom this book would never have happened.

I
Let Erin Remember

Lillibuléro

Thomas, 1st Marquis of Wharton

A song forever associated with James II and his attempt to retain the English throne by using the Irish. Tyrconnel was appointed Lord-Deputy and the song by Thomas, Marquis of Wharton, was the Protestant response. He boasted that it whistled James out of three kingdoms. The refrain is a mocking parody of the Catholic watchcry during their rising of 1641 and probably means *An lile bá léir é, ba linne an lá* (The lily prevailed; the day was ours.)

Ho brother Teig, dost hear the decree,
Lillibuléro bullen a la,
Dat we shall have a new Debittie,
Lillibuléro bullen a la.

Chorus
Lero lero lero lero,
Lillibuléro bullen a la,
Lillibuléro lero lero,
Lillibuléro bullen a la.

Ho, by my Soul, it is a Talbot;
   Lillibuléro, etc.
And he will cut all de English throat,
   Lillibuléro, etc.

Though, by my Soul, de English do prate,
   Lillibuléro, etc.
De Law's on dere side and de divil knows what,
   Lillibuléro, etc.

But if Dispence do come from the Pope,
 Lillibuléro, etc.
We'll hang Magna Cart and demselves in a rope,
 Lillibuléro, etc.

And the good Talbot is now made a Lord,
 Lillibuléro, etc.
And with his brave lads he's coming abroad,
 Lillibuléro, etc.

Who all in France have taken a swear,
 Lillibuléro, etc.
Dat day will have no Protestant heir.
 Lillibuléro, etc.

O but why does he stay behind?
 Lillibuléro, etc.
Ho, by my Soul, 'tis a Protestant wind,
 Lillibuléro, etc.

Now that Tyrconnel is come ashore,
 Lillibuléro, etc.
And we shall have Commissions *go leór*,
 Lillibuléro, etc.

And he dat will not go to the Mass,
 Lillibuléro, etc.
Shall be turned out and look like an ass.
 Lillibuléro, etc.

Now, now de hereticks all will go down,
 Lillibuléro, etc.
By Christ and St. Patrick the nation's our own.
 Lillibuléro, etc.

Dere was an old prophecy found in a bog,
  Lillibuléro, etc.
Dat our land would be ruled by an ass and a dog.
  Lillibuléro, etc.

So now dis old Prophecy's coming to pass,
  Lillibuléro bullen a la,
For James is de dog and Tyrconnel's de ass.
  Lillibuléro, etc.

The Battle of the Boyne

Anonymous

The battle was fought not as celebrated on 12 July but on the 1st at Oldbridge, downriver from Slane (the calendar was changed in 1752). It was the first and last confrontation of James and his rival, William III. James fled and the battle became the symbol of Orange Ascendancy. Because of French involvement on the Stuart side the battle was seen as a blow to the ambition of Louis XIV and Pope Alexander VIII was pleased to assent to a *Te Deum* being sung throughout Austria.

July the first, in Oldbridge town,
There was a grevious battle,
Where many a man lay on the ground,
By cannons that did rattle.
King James he pitched his tents between
The lines for to retire;
But King William threw his bomb-balls in,
And set them all on fire.

Thereat enraged they vowed revenge
Upon King William's forces,
And oft did vehemently cry
That they would stop their courses,
A bullet from the Irish came,
And grazed King William's arm,
They thought his majesty was slain,
Yet it did him little harm.

Duke Schomberg then, in friendly care,
His King would often caution,
To shun the spot where bullets hot

Retained their rapid motion;
But William said, he don't deserve
The name of Faith's defender,
Who would not venture life and limb
To make a foe surrender.

When we the Boyne began to cross,
The enemy they descended;
But few of our brave men were lost,
So stoutly we defended;
The horse was the first that marched o'er,
The foot soon followed after;
But brave Duke Schomberg was no more,
By venturing over the water.

When valiant Schomberg he was slain,
King William he accosted
His warlike men for to march on
And he would be the foremost;
"Brave boys," he said, "be not dismayed,
For the loss of one commander.
For God will be our king this day,
And I'll be general under."

Then stoutly we the Boyne did cross
To give the enemies battle;
Our cannon to our foe's great cost
Like thundering claps did rattle,
In majestic mien our Prince rode o'er,
His men soon followed after,
With blow and shout put our foes to the rout
The day we crossed the water.

The Protestants of Drogheda
Have reason to be thankful,
That they were not to bondage brought
They being but a handful,
First to the Tholsel they were brought,

And tried at the Millmount after;
But brave King William set them free,
By venturing over the water.

The cunning French near to Duleek
Had taken up their quarters,
And fenced themselves on every side
Still waiting for new orders;
But in the dead time of the night,
They set the field on fire,
And long before the morning light,
To Dublin they did retire.

Croppies Lie Down

Anonymous

The Loyalist answer to the various risings of 1798. It is one of
the finest pieces in the Orange canon. The unselfconscious
nationalism of the first line can only be evidence of early
Protestant *Sinn Féin*.

We soldiers of Erin, so proud of the name,
Will raise upon Rebels and Frenchmen our fame;
We'll fight to the last in the honest old cause,
And guard our religion, our freedom, and laws;
We'll fight for our country, our king, and his crown,
And make all the traitors and croppies lie down.

Down, down, croppies lie down.

The rebels so bold — when they've none to oppose —
To houses and hay-stacks are terrible foes;
They murder poor parsons, and also their wives,
But soldiers at once make them run for their lives;
And wherever we march, thro' the country or town,
In ditches or cellars, the croppies lie down.

United in blood, to their country's disgrace,
They secretly shoot whom they dare not to face;
But when we can catch the sly rogues in the field,
A handful of soldiers make hundreds to yield,
And the cowards collect but to raise our renown,
For as soon as we fire the croppies lie down.

While they, in the war that unmanly they wage
On woman herself turn their blood-thirsty rage,
We'll fly to protect the dear creatures from harms,

And shelter them safely when clasp'd in our arms:
On love in a soldier no maiden will frown,
But bless the dear boys that made croppies lie down.

Should France e'er attempt, or by fraud or by guile,
Her forces to land on our emerald isle,
We'll shew that they ne'er can make free soldiers slaves,
And only possess our green fields for their graves;
Our country's applauses our triumph will crown,
While low with the French, brother, croppies lie down.

When wars and when dangers again shall be o'er,
And peace with her blessings revisit our shore;
When arms we relinquish, no longer to roam,
With pride will our families welcome us home,
And drink, as in bumpers past troubles we drown,
A health to the lads that made croppies lie down.

The Wearing of the Green

Anonymous

One of the most evocative ballads of the period that followed 1798. Dion Boucicault used it in his play, *Arrah-na-Pogue*, so that he is sometimes taken to be the author, but the allusion to Napper Tandy, who died in 1802, indicates that it belongs to the early years of the nineteenth century.

O Paddy dear, and did ye hear the news that's goin' round?
The shamrock is by law forbid to grow on Irish ground!
No more Saint Patrick's Day we'll keep, his colour can't
    be seen,
For there's a cruel law ag'in the Wearin' o' the Green.
I met with Napper Tandy, and he took me by the hand,
And he said, "How's poor ould Ireland, and how does she
    stand?"
She's the most distressful country that ever yet was seen,
For they're hanging men and women there for the
    Wearin' o' the Green.

So if the colour we must wear be England's cruel red
Let it remind us of the blood that Irishmen have shed;
And pull the shamrock from your hat, and throw it on
    the sod,
But never fear, 'twill take root there, though underfoot
    'tis trod.
When laws can stop the blades of grass from growin' as
    they grow,
And when the leaves in summer-time their colour dare
    not show,
Then I will change the colour too I wear in my caubeen;
But till that day, please God, I'll stick to the Wearin' o'
    the Green.

Last Words

(before his execution on 20 September 1803)

Robert Emmet

Emmet's last words are famous for their eloquence and their elegance. The last paragraph was once part of every Nationalist's repertoire and the second-last sentence has become threadbare through overuse by every platform speaker needing to rouse a jaded audience.

My lords, as to why judgement of death and execution should not be passed on me, according to law, I have nothing to say; but as to why my character should not be relieved from the imputations and calumnies thrown out against it, I have much to say. I do not imagine that your lordships will give credit to what I am going to utter; I have no hopes that I can anchor my character in the breast of the court, I only wish your lordships may suffer it to float down your memories until it has found some more hospitable harbour to shelter it from the storms with which it is at present buffeted. Was I to suffer only death, after being adjudged guilty, I should bow in silence to the fate which awaits me; but the sentence of the law which delivers over my body to the executioner, consigns my character to obloquy. A man in my situation has not only to encounter the difficulties of fortune, but also the difficulties of prejudice. Whilst the man dies, his memory lives; and that mine may not forfeit all claim to the respect of my countrymen, I seize upon this opportunity to vindicate myself from some of the charges alleged against me. I am charged with being an emissary of France: it is false—I am no emissary. I do not wish to deliver up my country to a foreign power, and least of all, to France. Never did I entertain the remotest idea of establishing French power in Ireland. . .

Were the French to come as invaders or enemies uninvited by the wishes of the people, I should oppose them to the utmost of my strength. Yes! my countrymen, I should advise you to meet them upon the beach with a sword in one hand and a torch in the other.

My lords, will a dying man be denied the legal privilege of exculpating himself in the eyes of the community from a reproach thrown upon him during his trial, by charging him with ambition and attempting to cast away, for a paltry consideration, the liberties of his country, why then insult me, or rather, why insult justice, in demanding of me why sentence of death should not be pronounced against me? I know, my lords, that the form prescribes that you should put the question: the form also confers a right to answering. This, no doubt, may be dispensed with, and so might the whole ceremony of the trial, since sentence was already pronounced at the Castle before your jury were impaneled. Your lordships are but the priests of the oracle, and I submit, but I insist on the whole of the form.

(*Here Mr. Emmet paused, and the court desired him to proceed.*)

My lords, you are impatient for the sacrifice. The blood which you seek is not congealed by the artificial terrors which surround your victim—it circulates warmly and unruffled through its channels, and in a little time it will cry to heaven—be yet patient! I have but a few words more to say—I am going to my cold and silent grave—my lamp of life is nearly extinguished—I have parted with everything that was dear to me in this life, and for my country's cause with the idol of my soul the object of my affections. My race is run—the grave opens to receive me, and I sink into its bosom. I have but one request to ask at my departure from this world, it is the charity of its silence. Let no man write my epitaph; for as no man who knows my motives dare now vindicate them, let not prejudice or ignorance asperse them. Let them rest in obscurity and peace, my memory be left in oblivion, and my tomb remain uninscribed, until other times and other men can do justice to my character. When my country takes her place among the nations of the earth, then, and not till then, let my epitaph be written. I have done.

The Maiden City

Charlotte Elizabeth

One of two poems (the other is "No Surrender") written
during the nineteenth century about the Siege of Derry by the
Stuart forces (1688-9). The author was a lady tract-writer from
Kilkenny and had no doubt that her poems, written under the
pseudonym "Charlotte Elizabeth", helped preserve "the ould
cause" that gave Protestants "their freedom, religion and
laws".

Where Foyle his swelling waters
   Rolls northward to the main,
Here, Queen of Erin's daughters,
   Fair Derry fixed her reign;
A holy temple crowned her,
   And commerce graced her street,
A rampart wall was round her,
   The river at her feet;
And here she sat alone, boys,
   And, looking from the hill,
Vowed the Maiden on her throne, boys,
   Would be a Maiden still.

From Antrim crossing over,
   In famous eighty-eight,
A plumed and belted lover
   Came to the Ferry Gate:
She summoned to defend her
   Our sires—a beardless race—
They shouted No Surrender!
   And slammed it in his face.
Then, in a quiet tone, boys,
   They told him 'twas their will
That the Maiden on her throne, boys,
   Should be a Maiden still.

Next, crushing all before him,
　A kingly wooer came
(The royal banner o'er him
　Blushed crimson deep for shame);
He showed the Pope's commission,
　Nor dreamed to be refused;
She pitied his condition,
　But begged to stand excused.
In short, the fact is known, boys,
　She chased him from the hill,
For the Maiden on the throne, boys,
　Would be a Maiden still.

On our brave sires descending,
　'Twas then the tempest broke,
Their peaceful dwellings rending,
　'Mid blood, and flame, and smoke.
That hallowed grave-yard yonder
　Swells with the slaughtered dead—
O brothers! pause and ponder—
It was for *us* they bled;
And while their gift we own, boys—
　The fane that tops our hill—
Oh! the Maiden on her throne, boys,
　Shall be a Maiden still!

Nor wily tongue shall move us,
　Nor tyrant arm affright,
We'll look to One above us
　Who ne'er forsook the right;
Who will, may crouch and tender
　The birthright of the free,
But, brothers, No Surrender,
　No compromise for me!
We want no barrier stone, boys,
　Nor gates to guard the hill,
Yet the Maiden on her throne, boys,
　Shall be a Maiden still.

The Burial of Sir John Moore

Charles Wolfe

Wolfe's poem, once a standard recitation in schools, tells of the death of the commander of the Peninsular forces before Corunna in January 1809. The command was then taken by Wellesley (afterwards the Duke of Wellington, the famous reluctant Irishman).

Not a drum was heard, not a funeral note,
   As his corse to the ramparts we hurried;
Not a soldier discharged his farewell shot
   O'er the grave where our hero we buried.

We buried him darkly, at dead of night,
   The sods with our bayonets turning,
By the struggling moonbeam's misty light,
   And the lantern dimly burning.

No useless coffin enclosed his breast,
   Not in sheet nor in shroud we wound him;
But he lay like a warrior taking his rest,
   With his martial cloak around him.

Few and short were the prayers we said,
   And we spake not a word of sorrow;
But we steadfastly gazed on the face that was dead,
   And we bitterly thought of the morrow

We thought as we hollowed his narrow bed,
   And smoothed down his lonely pillow,
That the foe and the stranger would tread o'er his head,
   And we far away on the billow!

Lightly they'll talk of the spirit that's gone,
   And o'er his cold ashes upbraid him,—
But little he'll reck if they let him sleep on
   In a grave where a Briton has laid him.

But half of our heavy task was done,
   When the clock struck the hour for retiring,
And we heard the distant and random gun
   That the foe was sullenly firing.

Slowly and sadly we laid him down,
   From the field of his fame fresh and gory;
We carved not a line, and we raised not a stone—
   But we left him alone in his glory!

The Ballad of Henry Joy

Anonymous

Henry Joy McCracken, born in Belfast in 1767, was with Thomas Russell the founder of the northern arm of the United Irishmen in 1791. Arrested in 1796, he was released on bail and became commander of the insurgents at Antrim. After their defeat in June 1798, he hid out in the South Antrim hills but was captured and hanged in Belfast on 17 July the same year. The song is part of the Protestant nationalist tradition.

An Ulster man I am proud to be,
From the Antrim Glens I come,
Although I labour by the sea,
I have followed flag and drum.
I have heard the martial tramp of men,
I have watched them fight and die;
And it's well do I remember
When I followed Henry Joy.

I pulled my boat up from the sea,
I hid my sails away,
I hung my nets on a greenwood tree,
And I scanned the moonlit bay,
The Boys went out, and the Redcoats, too;
I kissed my wife goodbye,
And in the shade of the greenwood glade,
Sure I followed Henry Joy.

In Antrim Town the tyrant stood,
He tore our ranks with ball,
But with a cheer and a pike to clear,
We swept them o'er the wall.

Our pikes and sabres flashed that day,
We won, but lost, ah! why
No matter, lads, I fought beside,
And shielded Henry Joy.

Ah, lads, for Ireland's cause we fought
For home and sire we bled,
Tho' pikes were fed, still our hearts beat true,
And five to one lay dead,
But many a lassie mourned her lad,
And mother mourned her boy;
For youth was strong in that gallant throng,
Who followed Henry Joy.

In Belfast town they built a tree,
And the Redcoats mustered there;
I watched him come as the beat of the drum
Rolled out from the barrack square.
He kissed his sister, went aloft,
Then bade a last goodbye,
My soul he died, och, I turned and cried,
They had murdered Henry Joy.

Bold Phelim Brady, Bard of Armagh

Anonymous

A song traditionally associated with the undercover life of
Saint Oliver Plunkett when, from 1673 to 1679, he carried out
his duties as Archbishop of Armagh in a variety of disguises,
including that of an itinerant harper. He was hanged at Tyburn
during the Titus Oates anti-Catholic hysteria.

Oh! list to the lay of a poor Irish harper,
And scorn not the strains of his old withered hand,
But remember the fingers could once move sharper,
To raise the merry strains of his dear native land.

It was long before the Shamrock, our green isle's loved
     emblem,
Was crushed in its beauty 'neath the Saxon lion's paw,
I was called by the colleens of the village and valley,
Bold Phelim Brady, the Bard of Armagh.

How I long for to muse on the days of my boyhood,
Though four score and three years have flitted since then,
Still it gives sweet reflections, as every young joy should,
That merry-hearted boys make the best of old men.

At a pattern or fair I could twist my shillelagh,
Or trip through the jig with my brogues bound with straw,
Whilst all the pretty maidens around me assembled,
Loved Bold Phelim Brady, the Bard of Armagh.

Although I have travelled this wide world over,
Yet Erin's my home and a parent to me,
Then oh! let the ground that my old bones shall cover
Be cut from the soil that is trod by the free.

And when Sergeant Death in his cold arms shall embrace me,
O lull me to sleep with sweet Erin go bragh.
By the side of my Kathleen, my young wife, O place me,
Then forget Phelim Brady, the Bard of Armagh.

Dolly's Brae

Anonymous

An account of a savage confrontation between Catholic Rib-
bonmen and Orangemen in County Down on 12 July 1849.
Thirty Catholics were killed. The previous year the Orange-
men had not attempted to pass the Ribbonmen's blockade but
they were hailed as cowards by the usual malevolent stirrers
for the whole year afterwards and came prepared with guns
the next time.

'Twas on the 12th day of July, in the year of '49,
Ten hundreds of our Orangemen together did combine,
In the memory of King William, on that bright and
glorious day,
To walk all round Lord Roden's park, and right over
Dolly's Brae.

And when we came to Weirsbridge—wasn't that a glorious
sight,
To see so many Orangemen all willing for to fight,
To march all round the old remains, the music so sweetly
did play,
And the tune we played was "The Protestant Boys" right
over Dolly's Brae.

And as we walked along the road not fearing any harm,
Our guns all over our shoulders, and our broadswords in
our hands,
Until two priests came up to us, and to Mr. Speers did say,
"Come, turn your men the other road, and don't cross
Dolly's Brae."

Then out bespeaks our Orangemen, "Indeed we won't
    delay,
You have your men all gathered and in a manger lay;
Begone, begone, you Papist dogs, we'll conquer or we'll
    die,
And we'll let you see we're not afraid to cross over Dolly's
    Brae."

And when we came to Dolly's Brae they were lined on
    every side,
Praying for the Virgin Mary to be their holy guide;
We loosened our guns upon them and we gave them no
    time to pray,
And the tune we played was "The Protestant Boys" right
    over Dolly's Brae.

The priest he came, his hands he wrung, saying, "My brave
    boys, you're dead
Some holy water I'll prepare, to sprinkle on your heads;"
The Pope of Rome he did disown, his heart was grieveful
    sore,
And the Orange cry, as we passed by, was "Dolly's Brae
    no more".

Come all ye blind-led Papists, wherever that ye be,
Never bow down to priest or Pope, for them they will
    disown;
Never bow down to images, for God [you must] adore,
Come, join our Orange heroes, and cry "Dolly's Brae no
    more".

There was a damsel among them all, and one we shall
    adore,
For she wore the Orange around her head and cried
    "Dolly's Brae no more".
And if they ever come back again, we'll give them ten times
    more,
And we'll christen this "King William's Bridge", and cry
    "Dolly's Brae no more".

Oh! The Praties They Are Small Over Here

Anonymous

A song sometimes incorrectly assigned to the great potato famines of the mid-Forties. It was written later and is more expressive of Ireland's *recurring* rural poverty.

Oh! the Praties they are small over here—over here
Oh! the Praties they are small over here,
Oh! the Praties they are small, and we dug them in the fall,
And we ate them skins and all, full of fear—full of fear.

Oh! I wish that we were geese in the morn—in the morn,
Oh! I wish that we were geese in the morn,
Oh! I wish that we were geese, for they live and die at
      peace,
Till the hour of their decease, eatin corn—eatin corn.

Oh! we're down into the dust, over here—over here
Oh, we're down into the dust over here,
Oh! we're down into the dust, but the Lord in whom we
      trust,
Will soon give us crumb or crust over here—over here.

Old Skibbereen

Anonymous

A song to suit the most lugubrious taste in Irish ballads based on a recurring theme in nineteenth century history—eviction followed by forced emigration. Skibbereen was the home of the famous Fenian leader, O'Donovan Rossa.

Oh, father dear, I often hear you speak of Erin's Isle,
Her lofty scenes and valleys green, her mountains rude and
   wild,
They say it is a lovely land wherein a prince might dwell,
Oh, why did you abandon it? the reason to me tell.

Oh, son! I loved my native land with energy and pride,
Till a blight came o'er my crops—my sheep, my cattle died;
My rent and taxes were too high, I could not them redeem,
And that's the cruel reason that I left old Skibbereen.

Oh, well do I remember the bleak December day,
The landlord and the sheriff came to drive us all away;
They set my roof on fire with their cursed English spleen,
And that's another reason that I left old Skibbereen.

Your mother, too, God rest her soul, fell on the snowy
         ground,
She fainted in her anguish, seeing the desolation round,
She never rose, but passed away from life to mortal dream,
And found a quiet grave, my boy, in dear old Skibbereen.

And you were only two years old and feeble was your
      frame,
I could not leave you with my friends you bore your
      father's name—
I wrapt you in my cotamore at the dead of night unseen,
I heaved a sigh and bade good-bye, to dear old Skibbereen.

Oh, father dear, the day may come when in answer to the
      call
Each Irishman, with feeling stern, will rally one and all;
I'll be the man to lead the van beneath the flag so green,
When loud and high we'll raise the cry—"Remember
      Skibbereen".

The Shan Van Vocht

Anonymous

An amalgam of several versions of the ballad associated with
Wolfe Tone's attempt to land French soldiers at Bantry Bay
in December 1796. The *Sean-Bhean Bhocht* ("the poor old
woman") has stood ever since for Ireland at her most
sorrowful.

Oh! the French are on the sea,
  Says the Shan Van Vocht;
The French are on the sea,
  Says the Shan Van Vocht:
Oh! the French are in the Bay,
They'll be here without delay,
And the Orange will decay,
  Says the Shan Van Vocht.
    Oh! the French are in the Bay,
    They'll be here by break of day,
    And the Orange will decay,
      Says the Shan Van Vocht.

And where will they have their camp?
  Says the Shan Van Vocht;
Where will they have their camp?
  Says the Shan Van Vocht;
On the Curragh of Kildare,
The boys they will be there,
With their pikes in good repair,
  Says the Shan Van Vocht.
    To the Curragh of Kildare
    The boys they will repair,
    And Lord Edward will be there,
      Says the Shan Van Vocht.

Then what will the yeomen do?
  Says the Shan Van Vocht;
What will the yeomen do?
  Says the Shan Van Vocht;
What should the yeomen do
But throw off the Red and Blue,
And swear that they'll be true
    To the Shan Van Vocht?
      What should the yeomen do
      But throw off the red and blue,
      And swear that they'll be true
        To the Shan Van Vocht?

And what colour will they wear?
  Says the Shan Van Vocht;
What colour will they wear?
  Says the Shan Van Vocht;
What colour should be seen
Where our fathers' homes have been,
But our own immortal Green?
  Says the Shan Van Vocht.
      What colour should be seen
      Where our fathers' homes have been
      But our own immortal Green?
        Says the Shan Van Vocht.

And will Ireland then be free?
  Says the Shan Van Vocht;
Will Ireland then be free?
  Says the Shan Van Vocht;
Yes! Ireland shall be free,
From the centre to the sea;
Then hurrah for Liberty!
  Says the Shan Van Vocht.
      Yes! Ireland shall be free,
      From the centre to the sea:
      Then hurrah for Liberty!
        Says the Shan Van Vocht.

Tone is Coming Back Again

Thomas Francis Mullan

A song which was part of the *'98 Cantata* written in celebration of the hundredth anniversary of the Rising. The cycle contained ten songs and was revived again in 1948 on the 150th anniversary.

Cheer up, brave hearts, to-morrow's dawn will see us
    march again
Beneath old Erin's flag of green that ne'er has known a
    stain.
And ere our hands the sword shall yield or furled that
    banner be—
We swear to make our native land from tyrant's thraldom
    free!

Chorus
For Tone is coming back again, with legions o'er the wave,
The scions of Lord Clare's Brigade, the dear old land to
    save.
For Tone is coming back again, with legions o'er the wave,
The dear old land, the loved old land, the brave old land to
    save!

Though crouching minions preach to us to be the Saxon's
    slave,
We'll teach them all what pikes can do when hearts are true
    and brave.
Fling Freedom's banner to the breeze, let it float o'er land
    and sea—
We swear to make our native land from the tyrant's
    thraldom free!

Chorus

Young Dwyer 'mong the heath-clad hills of Wicklow leads
      his men;
And Russell's voice stirs kindred hearts in many an Ulster
      glen.
Brave Father Murphy's men march on from the Barrow to
      the sea—
We swear to make our native land from the tyrant's
      thraldom free!

Chorus

Too long we've borne with smouldering wrath the cursed
      alien laws,
That wreck our shrines and burn our homes and crush our
      country's cause;
But now the day has come at last; Revenge our watchword
      be!
We swear to make our native land from the tyrant's
      thraldom free!

Chorus

Dark Rosaleen

James Clarence Mangan

The most famous poem of the odd, early nineteenth century
poet whose staple diet was drink and dreams. He knew no
Irish but was friendly with O'Curry and O'Daly in the
Ordnance Survey Office and this version of *Roisin Dubh*
(Little Black Rose) is now as well known as the original.
"Roisin Dubh" is one of many soubriquets for Ireland.

> O my dark Rosaleen,
>   Do not sigh, do not weep!
> The priests are on the ocean green,
>   They march along the deep.
> There's wine from the royal Pope,
>   Upon the ocean green;
> And Spanish ale shall give you hope,
>   My Dark Rosaleen!
>   My own Rosaleen!
> Shall glad your heart, shall give you hope,
> Shall give you health, and help, and hope.
>   My Dark Rosaleen!

> Over hills, and thro' dales,
>   Have I roam'd for your sake;
> All yesterday I sail'd with sails
>   On river and on lake.
> The Erne, at its highest flood,
>   I dash'd across unseen,
> For there was lightning in my blood,
>   My Dark Rosaleen!

At home, in your emerald bowers,
　From morning's dawn till e'en,
You'll pray for me, my flower of flowers,
　My Dark Rosaleen!
　My fond Rosaleen!
You'll think of me through daylight hours,
My virgin flower, my flower of flowers,
　My Dark Rosaleen!

I could scale the blue air,
　I could plough the high hills,
Oh, I could kneel all night in prayer,
　To heal your many ills!
And one beamy smile from you
　Would float like light between
My toils and me, my own, my true,
　My Dark Rosaleen!
　My fond Rosaleen!
Would give me life and soul anew,
A second life, a soul anew,
　My Dark Rosaleen!

O, the Erne shall run red,
　With redundance of blood,
The earth shall rock beneath our tread,
　And flames wrap hill and wood,
And gun-peal and slogan-cry
　Wake many a glen serene,
Ere you shall fade, ere you shall die,
　My Dark Rosaleen!
　My own Rosaleen!
The Judgement Hour must first be nigh,
Ere you can fade, ere you can die,
　My Dark Rosaleen!

The West's Asleep

Thomas Davis

Thomas Davis's most popular poem which, set to quite remarkable music, moved even Yeats who was tone-deaf and properly critical of the *Nation's* verse as poetry. He said he could never hear it "without great excitement".

When all beside a vigil keep
The West's asleep, the West's asleep—
Alas! and well may Erin weep
When Connacht lies in slumber deep.
There lake and plain smile fair and free,
'Mid rocks their guardian chivalry.
Sing, Oh! let man learn liberty
From crashing wind and lashing sea.

That chainless wave and lovely land
Freedom and Nationhood demand;
Be sure, the great God never planned,
For slumb'ring slaves a home so grand.
And long, a brave and haughty race
Honoured and sentinelled the place.
Sing, Oh! not even their son's disgrace
Can quite destroy their glory's trace.

For often, in O'Connor's van,
To triumph dashed each Connacht clan.
And fleet as deer the Normans ran
Thro' Corrsliabh Pass and Ardrahan;
And later times saw deeds as brave,
And glory guards Clanricarde's grave,
Sing, Oh! they died their land to save
At Aughrim's slopes and Shannon's wave.

And if, when all a vigil keep,
The West's asleep; the West's asleep!
Alas! and well may Erin weep,
That Connacht lies in slumber deep,
But hark! a voice like thunder spake
"The West's awake! the West's awake!"
Sing, Oh! hurrah! let England quake,
We'll watch till death for Erin's sake!

The Memory of the Dead

John Kells Ingram

Better known by its first line, this poem was published in the
Nation anonymously in 1843. Its author became Professor of
Greek, Vice-Provost of Trinity and President of the Royal
Irish Academy, and though never a nationalist equally never
denied its authorship.

Who fears to speak of Ninety-eight?
Who blushes at the name?
When cowards mock the patriot's fate,
Who hangs his head for shame?
He's all a knave, or half a slave,
Who slights his country thus;
But a true man, like you, man,
Will fill your glass with us.

We drink the memory of the brave,
The faithful and the few;
Some lie far off beyond the wave,
Some sleep in Ireland, too;
All, all are gone; but still lives on
The fame of those who died;
All true men, like you, men,
Remember them with pride.

Some on the shores of distant lands
Their weary hearts have laid,
And by the stranger's heedless hands
Their lonely graves were made;
But though their clay be far away
Beyond the Atlantic foam,
In true men, like you, men,
Their spirit's still at home.

The dust of some is Irish earth,
Among their own they rest,
And the same land that gave them birth
Has caught them to her breast;
And we will pray that from their clay
Full many a race may start
Of true men, like you, men,
To act as brave a part.

They rose in dark and evil days
To right their native land;
They kindled here a living blaze
That nothing shall withstand.
Alas! that might can vanquish right—
They fell and passed away;
But true men, like you, men,
Are plenty here to-day.

Then here's their memory—may it be
For us a guiding light,
To cheer our strife for liberty,
And teach us to unite—
Through good and ill, be Ireland's still,
Though sad as theirs your fate,
And true men be you, men,
Like those of Ninety-eight.

O'Donnell Abu

Michael Joseph McCann

A typical *Nation* poem intended to revive a pride in the dormant country by recounting rare past successes. The tune used to be a call-signal for Radio Eireann.

Proudly the note of the trumpet is sounding,
Loudly the war-cries arise on the gale;
Fleetly the steed by Loch Suiligh is bounding,
To join the thick squadrons in Saimear's green vale,
On, every mountaineer,
Strangers to flight and fear,
Rush to the standards of dauntless Red Hugh!
Bonnought and gallowglass
Throng from each mountain pass!
On for old Erin—O'Donnell abu!

Princely O'Neill to our aid is advancing,
With many a chieftain and warrior clan;
A thousand proud steeds in his vanguard are prancing
'Neath the borders brave from the banks of the Bann—
Many a heart shall quail
Under its coat of mail,
Deeply the merciless foeman shall rue,
When on his ear shall ring,
Borne on the breeze's wing,
Tir-Conaill's dread war-cry—O'Donnell abu!

Wildly o'er Desmond the war-wolf is howling,
Fearless the eagle sweeps over the plain;
The fox in the streets of the city is prowling,
All, all who would scare them are banished or slain.
Grasp, every stalwart hand,
Hackbut and battle-brand,

Pay them all back the deep debt so long due;
Norris and Clifford well
Can Tir-Conaill tell—
Onward to glory—O'Donnell abu!

Sacred the cause that Clan-Conaill's defending,
The altars we kneel at, the homes of our sires;
Ruthless the ruin the foe is extending,
Midnight is red with the plunderers' fires!
On with O'Donnell then,
Fight the old fight again,
Sons of Tir Conaill, all valiant and true!
Make the false Saxon feel
Erin's avenging steel!
Strike for your country!—O'Donnell abu!

The Celts

Thomas D'Arcy McGee

A better than usual "remember the glories" poem, full of
nineteenth century romanticism and imprecise scholarship.
McGee was shot by former comrades for turning against the
Fenian movement.

> Long, long ago, beyond the misty space
>   Of twice a thousand years,
> In Erin old there dwelt a mighty race,
>   Taller than Roman spears;
> Like oaks and towers they had a giant grace,
>   Were fleet as deers,
> With wind and waves they made their 'biding place,
> These western shepherd seers.

> Their Ocean-God was Manannan MacLir,
>   Whose angry lips,
> In their white foam, full often would inter
>   Whole fleets of ships;
> Cromah their Day-God, and their Thunderer
>   Made morning and eclipse;
> Bride was their Queen of Song, and unto her
>   They prayed with fire-touched lips.

> Great were their deeds, their passions and their sports;
>   With clay and stone
> They piled on strath and shore those mystic forts,
>   Not yet o'erthrown;
> On cairn-crowned hills they held their council-courts;
>   While youths alone,
> With giant dogs, explored the elk resorts,
>   And brought them down.

Of these was Finn, the father of the Bard,
  Whose ancient song
Over the clamour of all change is heard,
  Sweet-voiced and strong.
Finn once o'ertook Grania, the golden-haired,
  The fleet and young;
From her the lovely, and from him the feared,
  The primal poet sprung.

Ossian! two thousand years of mist and change
  Surround thy name—
Thy Fenian heroes now no longer range
  The hills of fame.
The very names of Finn and Gaul sound strange—
  Yet thine the same—
By miscalled lake and desecrated grange—
  Remains, and shall remain!

The Druid's altar and the Druid's creed
  We scarce can trace,
There is not left an undisputed deed
  Of all your race,
Save your majestic song, which hath their speed,
  And strength and grace;
In that sole song, they live and love, and bleed—
  It bears them on through space.

O, inspired giant! shall we e'er behold,
  In our own time,
One fit to speak your spirit on the wold,
  Or seize your rhyme?
One pupil of the past, as mighty-souled
  As in the prime,
Were the fond, fair, and beautiful, and bold—
  They of your song sublime!

The Boys of Wexford

Robert Dwyer Joyce

No rising inspired so many ballads as that of 1798, especially when viewed from the comparative safety and peace of mid-nineteenth century. "The Boys of Wexford" is one of many happy marriages of words and music. The "yeos" were the loyal militia who helped put down the various outbreaks with great savagery.

In comes the captain's daughter, the captain of the Yeos,
Saying, "Brave United man, we'll ne'er again be foes.
A thousand pounds I'll give you, and fly from home with
    thee,
And dress myself in man's attire, and fight for libertie!"
We are the boys of Wexford, who fought with heart and
    hand
To burst in twain the galling chain, and free our native
    land!

"I want no gold, my maiden fair, to fly from home with
    thee;
Your shining eyes will be my prize—more dear than gold
    to me.
I want no gold to nerve my arm to do a true man's part—
To free my land I'd gladly give the red drops from my
    heart."
We are the boys of Wexford, who fought with heart and
    hand
To burst in twain the galling chain, and free our native
    land!

And when we left our cabins, boys, we left with right good
      will,
To see our friends and neighbours that were at Vinegar
      Hill!
A young man from our ranks, a cannon he let go;
He slapt it into Lord Mountjoy—a tyrant he laid low!
We are the boys of Wexford, who fought with heart and
      hand
To burst in twain the galling chain, and free our native
      land!

We bravely fought and conquered at Ross, and Wexford
      town;
And, if we failed to keep them, 'twas drink that brought us
      down.
We had no drink beside us on Tubberneering's day,
Depending on the long bright pike, and well it worked its
      way!
We are the boys of Wexford, who fought with heart and
      hand
To burst in twain the galling chain, and free our native
      land!

They came into the country our blood to waste and spill;
But let them weep for Wexford, and think of Oulart Hill!
'Twas drink that still betrayed us—of them we had no fear;
For every man could do his part like Forth and Shelmalier!
We are the boys of Wexford, who fought with heart and
      hand
To burst in twain the galling chain, and free our native
      land!

My curse upon all drinking! It made our hearts full sore;
For bravery won each battle, but drink lost ever more;
And if, for want of leaders, we lost at Vinegar Hill,
We're ready for another fight, and love our country still!
We are the boys of Wexford, who fought with heart and
      hand
To burst in twain the galling chain, and free our native
      land!

The Croppy Boy

(A Ballad of '98)

William McBurney

The subtitle, "A Ballad of '98", might read "*The* Ballad of
'98". It has been sung eternally since its composition in 1845,
in spite of very approximate rhymes; it has given Joseph
Tomelty a title for a play and runs through Jennifer Johnston's
novel, *How Many Miles to Babylon?*

"Good men and true! in this house who dwell,
To a stranger bouchal I pray you tell,
Is the priest at home? or may he be seen?
I would speak a word with Father Green."
"The priest's at home, boy, and may be seen:
'Tis easy speaking with Father Green:
But you must wait till I go and see
If the holy father alone may be."

The youth has entered an empty hall—
What a lonely sound has his light foot-fall!
And the gloomy chamber's chill and bare,
With a vested priest in a lonely chair.
The youth has knelt to tell his sins,
"Nomine Dei", the youth begins
At "Mea cupla", he beats his breast,
And in broken murmurs he speaks the rest.

"At the siege of Ross did my father fall,
And at Gorey my loving brothers all;
I alone am left of my name and race,
I will go to Wexford and take their place,
I cursed three times since last Easter day—

At Mass-time once I went to play;
I passed the churchyard one day in haste
And forgot to pray for my mother's rest.

"I bear no hate against living thing,
But I love my country above my King,
Now, Father! bless me and let me go,
To die, if God has ordained it so."
The priest said naught, but a rustling noise
Made the youth look up in wild surprise:
The robes were off, and in scarlet there
Sat a Yeoman captain with fiery glare.

With fiery glare and with fury hoarse,
Instead of a blessing he breathed a curse:—
"'Twas a good thought, boy, to come here and shrive,
For one short hour is your time to live."
"Upon yon river three tenders float,
The priest's in one—if he isn't shot—
We hold this house for our lord and King,
And, Amen, say I, may all traitors swing!"

At Geneva Barracks that young man died.
And at Passage they have his body laid,
Good people, who live in peace and joy,
Breathe a prayer, shed a tear for the Croppy Boy.

The Rising of the Moon

John Keegan Casey

Or is this *the* '98 ballad? Certainly it was sung as often and has the same tendency to invade even the most quiescent nationalist imagination. Casey wrote it out of the diehard spirit of Fenianism that has persisted in Ireland for good or ill to the present day.

> "O then, tell me, Shawn O'Farrell, tell me why you hurry
>   so?"
> "Hush, ma bouchal, hush and listen;" and his cheeks were
>   all a-glow:
> "I bear orders from the captain—get you ready quick and
>   soon;
> For the pikes must be together at the risin' of the Moon."

> "O then, tell me, Shawn O'Farrell, where the gath'rin' is to
>   be?"
> "In the old spot by the river, right well known to you and
>   me;
> One word more—for signal token, whistle up the marchin'
>   tune,
> With your pike upon your shoulder, by the risin' of the
>   Moon."

> Out from many a mud-wall cabin eyes were watching
>   through that night;
> Many a manly heart was throbbing for the blessed warning
>   light.
> Murmurs passed along the valleys, like the banshee's lonely
>   croon,
> And a thousand blades were flashing at the risin' of the
>   Moon.

There, beside the singing river, that dark mass of men was
      seen—
Far above the shining weapons hung their own beloved
      Green.
"Death to every foe and traitor! Forward! strike the
      marchin' tune,
And hurrah, my boys, for freedom! 'tis the risin' of the
      Moon."

Well they fought for poor old Ireland, and full bitter was
      their fate;
(O what glorious pride and sorrow fills the name of
      'Ninety-Eight!)
Yet, thank God, e'en still are beating hearts in manhood's
      burning noon,
Who would follow in their footsteps at the risin' of the
      Moon!

The Irish Colonel

Sir Arthur Conan Doyle

The King was Louis XV, the colonel a Wild Goose, and the epigram one of the pleasanter myths of the Wild Geese adventures that stretched from Tobruk to Belgrade.

> Said the king to the colonel,
> "The complaints are eternal,
> That you Irish give more trouble
> Than any other corps."
>
> Said the colonel to the king,
> "This complaint is no new thing,
> For your foemen have made it
> A hundred times before."

Boolavogue

Patrick Joseph McCall

Another famous '98 ballad of the Wexford rising written by one of the great balladeers of the turn of the century. Father Murphy from old Kilcormack is as famous as Rody McCorley and Kelly from Killane.

At Boolavogue, as the sun was setting,
O'er the bright May meadows of Shelmalier,
A rebel hand set the heather blazing
And brought the neighbours from far and near,
Then Father Murphy, from old Kilcormack,
Spurred up the rock with a warning cry;
"Arm! Arm!" he cried, "for I've come to lead you
For Ireland's freedom we fight or die."

He led us on 'gainst the coming soldiers,
And the cowardly yeomen we put to flight;
'Twas at the Harrow the boys of Wexford
Showed Bookey's regiment how men could fight.
Look out for hirelings, King George of England,
Search every kingdom where breathes a slave,
For Father Murphy of County Wexford
Sweeps o'er the land like a mighty wave.

We took Camolin and Enniscorthy,
And Wexford storming drove out our foes;
'Twas at Slieve Coillte our pikes were reeking
With the crimson stream of the beaten Yeos.
At Tubberneering and Ballyellis
Full many a Hessian lay in his gore;
Ah, Father Murphy, had aid come over
The green flag floated from shore to shore.

At Vinegar Hill, o'er the pleasant Slaney,
Our heroes vainly stood back to back;
And the Yeos at Tullow took Father Murphy
And burned his body upon the rack.
God grant your glory, brave Father Murphy,
And open Heaven to all your men;
The cause that called you may call to-morrow
In another fight for the Green again.

Marching Song of Fiach MacHugh

Patrick Joseph McCall

More commonly known as "Follow me up to Carlow". Fiach MacHugh O'Byrne was the chief of the O'Byrnes of Wicklow in the second half of the sixteenth century. He inflicted a severe defeat upon the forces of the Pale in 1580 and continued to harry the forces of succeeding Deputies including Fitzwilliam. He was captured in 1597 and beheaded.

Lift, MacCahir Og, your face,
   Brooding o'er the old disgrace
That black Fitzwilliam stormed your place
   And sent you to the fern!
Grey said victory was sure—
   Soon the fire brand he'd secure
Until he met at Glenmalure
   Fiach MacHugh O'Byrne!

Chorus
Curse and swear, Lord Kildare!
Fiach will do what Fiach will dare—
Now Fitzwilliam, have a care;
   Fallen is your star low!
Up with halbert, out with sword!
On we go; for, by the Lord!
Fiach MacHugh has given the word:
   "Follow me up to Carlow."

See the swords of Glen Imayle
Flashing o'er the English Pale!
See all the children of the Gael!
   Beneath O'Byrne's banners!
Rooster of fighting stock,

Would you let a Saxon cock
Crow out upon an Irish rock?
  Fly up, and teach him manners!

From Tassagart to Clonmore
Flows a stream of Saxon gore
Och, great is Rory Og O'More
  At sending loons to Hades!
White is sick, and Lane is fled!
Now for black Fitzwilliam's head—
We'll send it over dripping red
  To Liza and her ladies!

Rody McCorley

Ethna Carbery

Another ballad of '98 written by Anna Johnston from Bally-
mena. Her hero, Rody McCorley, had been prominent in the
battle of Antrim in June 1798 and was hanged at Toomebridge
soon afterwards.

Ho! see the hosts of fleetfoot men
Who speed with faces wan,
From farmstead and from fishers' cot
Upon the banks of Bann.
They come with vengeance in their eyes
Too late, too late are they.
For Rody McCorley goes to die
On the bridge of Toome to-day.

Oh! Ireland, mother Ireland,
You love them still the best,
The fearless brave who fighting fall
Upon your hapless breast.
But never a one of all your dead
More bravely fell in fray
Then he who marches to his fate
On the bridge of Toome to-day.

Up the narrow street he stepped
Smiling and proud and young
About the hemp-rope on his neck
The golden ringlets clung;
There's never a tear in the blue eyes
Both glad and bright are they,
As Rody McCorley goes to die
On the bridge of Toome to-day.

Because he loved the motherland,
Because he loved the green
He goes to meet the martyr's fate
With proud and joyous mien;
True to the last, oh! true to the last
He treads the upward way;
Young Rody McCorley goes to die
On the bridge of Toome to-day.

Bold Robert Emmet

Thomas Maguire

One of the great nineteenth century ballads on Ireland's single most popular insurgent hero. It was written by Thomas Maguire who was an authentic balladeer who sang and sold his own songs at fairs and on street corners.

The struggle is over, the boys are defeated,
Old Ireland's surrounded with sadness and gloom;
We were defeated and shamefully treated,
And I, Robert Emmet awaiting my doom.
Hung, drawn and quartered, sure that was my sentence,
But soon I will show them no coward am I;
My crime is the love of the land I was born in,
A hero I lived and a hero I'll die.

Chorus
Bold Robert Emmet, the darling of Erin,
Bold Robert Emmet will die with a smile;
Farewell companions both loyal and daring,
I'll lay down my life for the Emerald Isle.

The barque lay at anchor awaiting to bring me
    Over the billows to the land of the free;
But I must see my sweetheart for I know she will cheer me,
    And with her I will sail far over the sea.
But I was arrested and cast into prison,
    Tried as a traitor, a rebel, a spy;
But no one can call me a knave or a coward,
    A hero I lived and a hero I'll die.

Chorus

Hark! the bell's tolling, I well know its meaning,
  My poor heart tells me it is my death knell;
In come the clergy, the warder is leading,
  I have no friends here to bid me farewell.
Good-bye, old Ireland, my parents and sweetheart,
  Companions in arms to forget you must try;
I am proud of the honour, it was only my duty—
  A hero I lived and a hero I'll die.

Chorus

The Men of the West

William Rooney

A ballad of the Year of the French written for the *Shamrock* by the co-founder (with Arthur Griffith) of the *United Irishman*.

While we honour in song and in story the names of the
    patriot men,
Whose valour has covered with glory full many a mountain
    and glen.
Forget not the boys of the heather, who marshalled their
    bravest and best,
When Eire was broken in Wexford and looked for revenge
    to the West.

Chorus
I give you "The Gallant old West", boys,
Where rallied our bravest and best,
When Ireland lay broken and bleeding,
Hurrah for the men of the West!

The hilltops with glory were glowing, 'twas the eve of a
    bright harvest day,
When the ships we'd been wearily waiting sailed into
    Killala's broad bay;
And over the hills went the slogan, to waken in every
    breast,
The fire that has never been quenched, boys, among the
    true hearts of the West.

Chorus

Killala was ours ere the midnight and high over Ballina
town,
Our banners in triumph were waving before the next sun
had gone down.
We gathered to speed the good work, boys, the true men
anear and afar;
And history can tell how we routed the redcoats through
old Castlebar.

Chorus

And pledge me "The stout sons of France", boys, bold
Humbert and all his brave men,
Whose tramp, like the trumpet of battle, brought hope to
the drooping again.
Since Eire has caught to her bosom on many a mountain
and hill,
The gallants who fell so they're here, boys, to cheer us to
victory still.

Chorus

Though all the bright dreamings we cherished went down
in disaster and woe,
The spirit of old is still with us that never would bend to
the foe;
And Connacht is ready whenever the loud rolling tuck of
the drum
Rings out to awaken the echoes and tell us—the morning
has come.

Chorus

So here's to "The Gallant old West", boys,
Who rallied her bravest and best,
When Ireland was broken and bleeding,
Hurrah, boys! Hurrah for the West!

Panegyric at the
Graveside of O'Donovan Rossa
(1 August 1915)

Patrick Pearse

One of the great pieces of Irish Volunteer rhetoric, part of a carefully prepared campaign in the year leading up to the Easter Rising. The piece is typically Pearsean with fine words and just accreditation of the Movement to the Fenian tradition. Though it is quoted (or used to be) as often as Robert Emmet's speech from the dock, Pearse's actual delivery at the graveside was poor, and his tribute to the Fenian hero was not heard beyond the first row of spectators.

It has seemed right, before we turn away from this place in which we have laid the mortal remains of O'Donovan Rossa, that one among us should, in the name of all, speak the praise of that valiant man, and endeavour to formulate the thought and the hope that are in us as we stand around his grave. And if there is anything that makes it fitting that I, rather than some other, I rather than one of the grey-haired men who were young with him and shared in his labour and in his suffering, should speak here, it is perhaps that I may be taken as speaking on behalf of a new generation that has been re-baptised in the Fenian faith, and that has accepted the responsibility of carrying out the Fenian programme. I propose to you then that, here by the grave of this unrepentant Fenian, we renew our baptismal vows; that, here by the grave of this unconquered and unconquerable man, we ask of God, each one for himself, such unshakable purpose, such high and gallant courage, such unbreakable strength of soul as belonged to O'Donovan Rossa.

Deliberately here we avow ourselves, as he avowed himself

in the dock, Irishmen of one allegiance only. We of the Irish Volunteers, and you others who are associated with us in to-day's task and duty, are bound together and must stand together henceforth in brotherly union for the achievement of the freedom of Ireland. And we know only one definition of freedom: it is Tone's definition, it is Mitchel's definition, it is Rossa's definition. Let no man blaspheme the cause that the dead generations of Ireland served by giving it any other name and definition than their name and their definition.

We stand at Rossa's grave not in sadness but rather in exaltation of spirit that it has been given to us to come thus into so close a communion with that brave and splendid Gael. Splendid and holy causes are served by men who are them-selves splendid and holy. O'Donovan Rossa was splendid in the proud manhood of him, splendid in the heroic grace of him, splendid in the Gaelic strength and clarity and truth of him. And all that splendour and pride and strength was compatible with a humility and a simplicity of devotion to Ireland, to all that was olden and beautiful and Gaelic in Ireland, the holiness and simplicity of patriotism of a Michael O'Clery or of an Eoghan O'Growney. The clear true eyes of this man almost alone in his day visioned Ireland as we of to-day would surely have her: not free merely, but Gaelic as well; not Gaelic merely, but free as well.

In a closer spiritual communion with him now than ever before or perhaps ever again, in a spiritual communion with those of his day, living and dead, who suffered with him in English prisons, in communion of spirit too with our own dear comrades who suffer in English prisons to-day, and speaking on their behalf as well as our own, we pledge to Ireland our love, and we pledge to English rule in Ireland our hate. This is a place of peace, sacred to the dead, where men should speak with all charity and with all restraint; but I hold it a Christian thing, as O'Donovan Rossa held it, to hate evil, to hate untruth, to hate oppression, and, hating them, to strive to overthrow them. Our foes are strong and wise and wary:

but, strong and wise and wary as they are, they cannot undo the miracles of God who ripens in the hearts of young men the seeds sown by the young men of a former generation. And the seeds sown by the young men of '65 and '67 are coming to their miraculous ripening to-day. Rulers and Defenders of Realms had need to be wary if they would guard against such processes. Life springs from death; and from the graves of patriot men and women spring living nations. The Defenders of this Realm have worked well in secret and in the open. They think that they have pacified Ireland. They think that they have purchased half of us and intimidated the other half. They think that they have foreseen everything, think that they have provided against everything; but the fools, the fools, the fools!—they have left us our Fenian dead, and while Ireland holds these graves, Ireland unfree shall never be at peace.

The Man from God-Knows-Where

Florence Wilson

A recitation written in nineteenth century Ulster dialect by a
County Down poet who died in Bangor in 1947. The man
was Thomas Russell who, with Henry Joy McCracken,
founded the northern arm of the United Irishmen in 1791.

Into our townlan', on a night of snow,
Rode a man from God-knows-where;
None of us bade him stay or go,
Nor deemed him friend, nor damned him foe,
But we stabled his big roan mare:
For in our townlan' we're decent folk,
And if he didn't speak, why none of us spoke,
And we sat till the fire burned low.

We're a civil sort in our wee place,
So we made the circle wide
Round Andy Lemon's cheerful blaze,
And wished the man his length of days,
And a good end to his ride.
He smiled in under his slouchy hat—
Says he: "There's a bit of a joke in that,
For we ride different ways."

The whiles we smoked we watched him stare
From his seat fornenst the glow.
I nudged Joe Moore: "You wouldn't dare
To ask him, who he's for meeting there,
And how far he has got to go."
But Joe wouldn't dare, nor Wully Scott,
And he took no drink—neither cold nor hot—
This man from God-knows-where.

It was closin' time, an' late forbye,
When us ones braved the air—
I never saw worse (may I live or die)
Then the sleet that night, an' I says, says I:
"You'll find he's for stopping there."
But at screek o' day, through the gable pane,
I watched him spur in the peltin' rain,
And I juked from his rovin' eye.

Two winters more, then the Trouble Year,
When the best that a man can feel
Was the pike he kept in hidin's near,
Till the blood 'o hate an' the blood o' fear
Would be redder nor rust on the steel.
Us ones quet from mindin' the farms,
Let them take what we gave wi' the weight o' our arms
From Saintfield to Kilkeel.

In the Time o' the Hurry, we had no lead—
We all of us fought with the rest—
An' if e'er a one shook like a tremblin' reed,
None of us gave neither hint nor heed.
Nor ever even'd we'd guessed.
We men of the North had a word to say,
An' we said it then, in our own dour way,
An' we spoke as we thought was best.

All Ulster over, the weemen cried
For the stan'-in' crops on the lan'—
Many's the sweetheart an' many's the bride
Would liefer ha' gone till where He died,
An ha' mourned her lone by her man.
But us ones weathered the thick of it,
And we used to dander along, and sit,
In Andy's, side by side.

What with discoorse goin' to and fro,
The night would be wearin' thin,
Yet never so late when we rose to go
But someone would say: "Do ye min' thon snow,
An' the man who came wanderin' in?"
And we be to fall the talk again,
If by any chance he was One O' Them—
The man who went like the win'.

Well 'twas gettin' on past the heat o' the year
When I rode to Newtown fair:
I sold as I could the dealers were near—
Only three pounds eight for the Innish steer,
(An' nothin' at all for the mare!)
I met M'Kee in the throng o' the street,
Says he: "The grass has grown under our feet
Since they hanged young Warwick here."

And he told me that Boney had promised help
To a man in Dublin town.
Says he: "If ye've laid the pike on the shelf,
Ye'd better go home hot-fut by yerself,
An' once more take it down."
So by Comber road I trotted the grey
And never cut corn until Killyleagh
Stood plain on the rising groun'.

For a wheen o' days we sat waitin' the word
To rise and go at it like men.
But no French ships sailed into Cloughey Bay,
And we heard the black news on a harvest day
That the cause was lost again;
And Joey and me, and Wully Boy Scott,
We agreed to ourselves we'd as lief as not
Ha' been found in the thick o' the slain.

By Downpatrick gaol I was bound to fare
On a day I'll remember, feth,
For when I came to the prison square
The people were waitin' in hundreds there,
An' you wouldn't hear stir nor breath!
For the sodgers were standing, grim an' tall,
Round a scaffold built there fornent the wall.
An' a man stepped out for death!

I was brave an' near to the edge of the throng,
Yet I knowed the face again.
An' I knowed the set, an' I knowed the walk
An' the sound of his strange up-country talk,
For he spoke out right an' plain.
Then he bowed his head to the swinging rope,
Whiles I said "Please God" to his dying hope
And "Amen" to his dying prayer,
That the Wrong would cease and the Right prevail,
For the man that they hanged at Downpatrick Gaol
Was the Man from GOD-KNOWS-WHERE!

Easter 1916
Proclamation of the Irish Republic

One of the sacred texts of the 1916 Rising. Written by Pearse with assistance from MacDonagh, it was read out at the General Post Office at the start of Easter Week. The first signatory was the veteran Thomas Clarke who was given the honour because of his long service to the cause.

Poblacht na hEireann
The Provisional Government of
The Irish Republic to
The People of Ireland

Irishmen and Irishwomen:

In the Name of God and of the dead generations from which she receives her old tradition of nationhood, Ireland, through us, summons her children to her flag and strikes for her freedom.

Having Organised and trained her manhood through her secret revolutionary organisation, the Irish Republican Brotherhood, and through her open military organisations, the Irish Volunteers and the Irish Citizen Army, having patiently perfected her discipline, having resolutely waited for the right moment to reveal itself, she now seizes that moment, and, supported by her exiled children in America and by gallant allies in Europe, but relying in the first on her own strength, she strikes in full confidence of victory.

We declare the right of the people of Ireland to the ownership of Ireland, and to the unfettered control of Irish destinies, to be sovereign and indefeasible. The long usurpation of that right by a foreign people and government has not extinguished the right, nor can it ever be extinguished except by the destruction of the Irish people. In every generation the

Irish have asserted their right to National freedom and sovereignty; six times during the past three hundred years they have asserted it in arms. Standing on that fundamental right and again asserting it in arms in the face of the world, we hereby proclaim the Irish Republic as a Sovereign Independent State, and we pledge our lives and the lives of our comrades-in-arms to the cause of its freedom, of its welfare, and of its exaltation among the nations.

The Irish Republic is entitled to, and hereby claims, the allegiance of every Irishman and Irishwoman. The Republic guarantees religious and civil liberty, equal rights and equal opportunities to all its citizens, and declares its resolve to pursue the happiness and prosperity of the whole nation and of all its parts, cherishing all the children of the nation equally, and oblivious of the differences carefully fostered by an alien government, which have divided a minority from the majority in the past.

Until Our Arms have brought the opportune moment for the establishment of a permanent National Government, representative of the whole people of Ireland and elected by the suffrages of all her men and women, the Provisional Government, hereby constitued, will administer the civil and military affairs of the Republic in trust for the people.

We place the cause of the Irish Republic under the protection of the Most High God, Whose blessing we invoke upon our arms, and we pray that no one who serves that cause will dishonour it by cowardice, inhumanity, or rapine. In this supreme hour the Irish nation must, by its valour and discipline and by the readiness of its children to sacrifice themselves for the common good, prove itself worthy of the august destiny to which it is called.

Signed on Behalf of the Provisional Government,

Thomas J. Clarke	Eamonn Ceannt
Sean MacDiarmada	James Connolly
Thomas MacDonagh	Joseph Plunkett
P. H. Pearse	

Solemn League and Covenant

The Loyalist oath, as central a part of Unionist theology as the Proclamation of 1916 is for republicans, was devised by Carson and Craig and signed by at least 200,000 Ulstermen on 28 September 1912.

Being convinced in our consciences that Home Rule would be disastrous to the material well-being of Ulster as well as of the whole of Ireland, subversive of our civil and religious freedom, destructive of our citizenship and perilous to the unity of the Empire, we, whose names are underwritten, men of Ulster, loyal subjects of His Gracious Majesty King George V.. humbly relying on the God whom our fathers in days of stress and trial confidently trusted, do hereby pledge ourselves in solemn Covenant throughout this our time of threatened calamity to stand by one another in defending for ourselves and our children our cherished position of equal citizenship in the United Kingdom and in using all means which may be found necessary to defeat the present conspiracy to set up a Home Rule Parliament in Ireland. ¶ And in the event of such a Parliament being forced upon us we further solemnly and mutually pledge ourselves to refuse to recognise its authority. ¶ In sure confidence that God will defend the right we hereto subscribe our names. ¶ And further, we individually declare that we have not already signed this Covenant.

The above was signed by me at .... "Ulster Day," Saturday, 28th September, 1912.

God Save the King.

II
The Ireland in the Heart

The Irish Dancer

Anonymous

A famous piece modernised by Yeats (among others). It is
dated 1300-1350 by John E. Wells, an authority on Middle
English, and is one of the earliest English dance-songs extant.

> I am of Ireland,
> And of the holy land
>   Of Ireland.
> Good sir, pray I thee,
> For of saint charity,
> Come and dance with me
>   In Ireland.

Ireland Delineated

Justice Luke Gernon

A prose-poem written by a justice in the early seventeenth century that is only just a little flattering.

Ireland is at all poynts like a young wench that hath a green sickness ... She is very fayre of visage, and hath a smooth skinn of tender grasse. Indeed she is somewhat freckled (as the Irish are) some partes darker than others. Her flesh is of a softe and delicate mould of earth, and her blew vaynes trayling through every part of her like rivulets. She hath one master vayne called the Shannon, which passeth quite through her, and if it were not for one knot (one mayne rock) it were navigable from head to foot. She hath three other vaynes called the sisters—the Suir, the Nore and the Barrow which, rising at one spring, trayle through her middle parts and joyne together in their going out.

Her bones are of polished marble, the grey marble, the black, the redd, and the speckled, so fayre for building that their houses show like colledges, and being polished, is most rarely embellished. Her breasts are round hillockes of milk-yielding grasse, and that so fertile, that they contend with the vallyes ... Of complexion she is very temperate, never too hott, nor too could, and hath a sweet breath of favonian winde.

She is of gentle nature. If the anger of heaven be agaynst her, she will not bluster and storme, but she will weep many days together, and (alas) this summer she did so water her plants that the grass and the blade was so bedewed, that it became unprofitable, and threatens a scarcity.

I Am Raftery

Anthony Raftery

Translated by Douglas Hyde

Ascribed to Antoine Ó Reachtabhra, the blind Mayo poet, who wrote the great song to Spring, "Anois teacht an Earraigh". The translation is one of many Connacht poems done by An Craoibhín Aoibhinn.

I AM Raftery the poet,
Full of hope and love,
With eyes that have no light,
With gentleness that has no misery.

Going west upon my pilgrimage
By the light of my heart,
Feeble and tired
To the end of my road.

Behold me now,
And my face to a wall,
A-playing music
Unto empty pockets.

Protestant Boys

Anonymous

One of several excellent rallying-cries which date from the late eighteenth century. The Orange Order was not founded until 1795, when it grew out of the Peep-of-Day Boys, but the Orange label from the house of the "saviour" William III was in free use before that.

TELL me, my friends, why are we met here?
    Why thus assembled, ye Protestant Boys?
Do mirth and good liquor, good humour, good cheer,
    Call us to share of festivity's joys?
          Oh, no! 'tis the cause
          Of king, "freedom," and laws,
That calls loyal Protestants now to unite;
          And Orange and Blue,
          Ever faithful and true,
Our king shall support, and sedition affright.

Great spirit of William! from heaven look down,
    And breathe in our hearts our forefathers' fire—
Teach us to rival their glorious renown,
    From Papist or Frenchman ne'er to retire.
          Jacobin—Jacobite—
          Against all to unite,
Who dare to assail our sovereign's throne?
          For Orange and Blue
          Will be faithful and true,
And Protestant loyalty ever be shown.

In that loyalty proud let us ever remain,
    Bound together in truth and religion's pure band;
Nor honor's fair cause with foul bigotry stain,

Since in courage and justice supported we stand
So heaven shall smile
On our emerald isle,
And lead us to conquest again and again;
While Papists shall prove
Our brotherly love;—
We hate them as masters—we love them as men.

By the deeds of their fathers to glory inspired,
Our Protestant heroes shall combat the foe;
Hearts with true honor and loyalty fired,
Intrepid, undaunted, to conquest will go.
In Orange and Blue,
Still faithful and true,
The soul-stirring music of glory they'll sing;
The shades of the Boyne
In the chorus will join,
And the welkin re-echo with God save the king.

The Green Little Shamrock

Andrew Cherry

Part of the (regretted by some) soft side of sentimental Ireland, this song was written for Cherry's play of the same name, at a time when such songs were a part of the normal decoration of English drama.

There's a dear little plant that grows in our isle;
'Twas St. Patrick himself sure that set it;
And the sun on his labour with pleasure did smile,
And with dew from his eye often wet it.
It thrives through the bog, through the brake and the
       mireland;
And he called it the dear little Shamrock of Ireland,
The sweet little shamrock, the dear little shamrock,
The sweet little, green little, shamrock of Ireland!

This dear little plant still grows in our land,
Fresh and fair as the daughters of Erin,
Whose smiles can bewitch, whose eyes can command,
In each climate that they may appear in;
And shine through the bog, through the brake and the
       mireland;
Just like their own dear little shamrock of Ireland,
The sweet little shamrock, the dear little shamrock,
The sweet little, green little, shamrock of Ireland!

This dear little plant that springs from our soil,
When its three little leaves are extended,
Denotes on one stalk we together should toil,
And ourselves by ourselves be befriended.
And still through the bog, through the brake and the
       mireland;
From one root should branch, like the shamrock of Ireland,
The sweet little shamrock, the dear little shamrock,
The sweet little, green little, shamrock of Ireland!

The Minstrel Boy

Thomas Moore

This stirring song, forever associated with its author (indeed
the title of one of his biographies), was one of several inspired
by the romantic and unsuccessful rising of his fellow Trinity
undergraduate, Robert Emmet.

The Minstrel Boy to the war is gone,
In the ranks of the dead you'll find him;
His father's sword he has girded on.
And his wild harp slung behind him.
"Land of song", said the warrior bard,
'Though all the world betray thee,
One sword, at least, thy rights shall guard,
One faithful harp shall praise thee."

The Minstrel fell—but the foeman's chain
Could not bring his proud soul under;
The harp he lov'd ne'er spoke again,
For he tore its chords asunder;
And said, "No chains shall sully thee,
Thou soul of love and bravery.
Thy songs were made for the pure and free,
They shall never sound in slavery."

She Is Far From the Land

Thomas Moore

Emmet would certainly have escaped to France, where he would again have been made welcome, had it not been for his consistent romanticism in visiting his sweetheart, Sarah Curran, at her house at Harold's Cross. Here he was captured by the efficient Major Sirr who earlier had taken Lord Edward Fitzgerald. Moore wrote the song in honour of Sarah Curran but the tune to which it is now customarily sung was not one of Moore's original *Melodies*.

> She is far from the land where her young hero sleeps,
>   And lovers are round her sighing;
> But coldly she turns from their gaze and weeps,
>   For her heart in his grave is lying!
>
> She sings the wild song of her dear native plains,
>   Every note which he loved awaking;
> Ah! little they think, who delight in her strains,
>   How the heart of the minstrel is breaking!
>
> He had lived for his love, for his country he died;
>   They were all that to life had entwined him;
> Nor soon shall the tears of his country be dried,
>   Nor long will his love stay behind him!
>
> Oh! make her a grave where the sunbeams rest
>   When they promise a glorious morrow;
> They'll shine o'er her sleep, like a smile from the west,
>   From her own loved island of sorrow.

The Orange Lily-o

Anonymous

An Orange song which in confidence and gaiety easily out-
distances those of the other tradition—small wonder in the
light of the historical situation. The most interesting point,
now ignored, is the strong nationalist air.

Oh did you go to see the show,
    Each rose an pink a dilly-o,
To feast your eyes upon the prize,
    Won by the Orange Lily-o.
The Viceroy there so debonair,
    Just like a daffy dilly-o
And Lady Clarke, blithe as a lark,
    Approached the Orange Lily-o

Chorus
Then heigh-o the Lily-o,
    The royal loyal Lily-o.
Beneath the sky what flower can vie,
    With Ireland's Orange Lily-o.

The elated muse, to hear the news,
    Jumped like a Connacht filly-o,
As gossip fame did loud proclaim
    The triumph of the Lily-o;
The lowland field may roses yield,
    Gay heaths the highlands hilly-o,
But high or low, no flower can show,
    Like the glorious Orange Lily-o.

Then heigho the lily-o,
    The royal, loyal lily-o.
There's not a flower in Erin's bower
    Can match the Orange Lily-o.

The Sash My Father Wore

Anonymous

Nowadays the best known of the Orange songs but in fact originating in Scotland. In fact the sash was not worn at any of the battles mentioned and nowadays is rarely seen at the sites of the second and fourth of the battles named.

Sure I'm an Ulster Orangeman, from Erin's Isle I came
To see my Glasgow brethren all of honour and of fame,
And to tell them of my forefathers who fought in days of
      yore,
All on the twelfth day of July in the sash my father wore.

Chorus
It's ould, but it's beautiful, and its colours they are fine,
It was worn at Derry, Aughrim, Enniskillen and the
      Boyne;
My father wore it in his youth in the bygone days of yore,
And on the Twelfth I love to wear the sash my father wore.

So here I am in Glasgow town youse boys and girls to see,
And I hope that in good Orange style you all will welcome
      me,
A true blue blade that's just arrived from that dear Ulster
      shore,
All on the Twelfth day of July in the sash my father wore.

Chorus

And when I'm going to leave yeeze all "Good luck!" to
      youse I'll say,
And as I cross the raging sea my Orange flute I'll play;
Returning to my native town, to ould Belfast once more,
To be welcomed back by Orangemen in the sash my father
      wore.

Chorus

Song for July 12th, 1843

Jean de Jean Fraser

One of several songs of reconciliation which the *Nation* published under the ecumenical influence of Thomas Davis.

Come—pledge again thy heart and hand—
   One grasp that ne'er shall sever;
Our watchword be— "Our native land"—
   Our motto—"Love for ever."
And let the Orange lily be
   Thy badge, my patriot brother—
The everlasting Green for *me;*
   And we for one another.

Behold how green the gallant stem
   On which the flower is blowing;
How in one heavenly breeze and beam
   Both flower and stem are glowing.
The same good soil, sustaining both,
   Makes both united flourish;
But cannot give the Orange growth,
   And cease the Green to nourish.

Yea, more—the hand that plucks the flow'r
   Will vainly strive to cherish;
The stem blooms on—but in that hour
   The flower begins to perish.
Regard them, then, of equal worth
   While lasts their genial weather;
The time's at hand when into earth
   The two shall sink together.

Ev'n thus be, in our country's cause,
   Our party feelings blended;
Till lasting peace, from equal laws,
   On both shall have descended.
Till then the Orange lily be
   Thy badge, my patriot brother—
The everlasting Green for *me;*
   And—we for one another.

A Nation Once Again

Thomas Davis

After "The West's Asleep" Davis's best song. The three men
of line four are Horatius, Herminius and Lartius who kept
the bridge against the Tuscan armies of Lars Porsena while
the three hundred are the Spartans under Leonidas who held
back the might of the Persian host at Thermopylae.

When boyhood's fire was in my blood
   I read of ancient freemen
For Greece and Rome who bravely stood—
   Three hundred men and three men.
And then I prayed I yet might see
   Our fetters rent in twain,
And Ireland, long a province, be
   A Nation once again.

And from that time, through wildest woe,
   That hope has shone, a far light,
Nor could love's brightest summer glow
   Outshine that solemn starlight:
It seemed to watch above my head
   In forum, field and fane;
Its angel voice sang round my bed
   "A Nation once again."

It whispered, too, that Freedom's ark
   And service high and holy,
Would be profaned by feelings dark
   And passions vain and lowly:
For Freedom comes from God's right hand,
   And needs a godly train;
And righteous men must make our land
   A Nation once again.

And as I grew from boy to man
    I bent me to that bidding—
My spirit of each selfish plan
    And cruel passion ridding;
For thus I hoped some day to aid—
    Oh, *can* such hope be vain?—
When my dear country shall be made
    A Nation once again.

God Save Ireland

T. D. Sullivan

Sullivan's song to a tune originally Irish but returning home as a Yankee marching song was dedicated to the Manchester Martyrs, Allen, Larkin and O'Brien, who were hanged for their part in the killing of Sergeant Brett during the attempt to rescue Fenian prisoners from Manchester Gaol in September 1867.

High upon the gallows tree swung the noble-hearted Three.
By the vengeful tyrant stricken in their bloom;
But they met him face to face, with the courage of their
      race,
And they went with souls undaunted to their doom.

Chorus
"God save Ireland!" said the heroes;
"God save Ireland!" said they all.
"Whether on the scaffold high
Or the battlefield we die,
O, what matter when for Erin dear we fall!"

Girt around with cruel foes, still their courage proudly
      rose,
For they thought of hearts that loved them far and near;
Of the millions true and brave o'er the ocean's swelling
      wave,
And the friends in holy Ireland ever dear.

Chorus

Climbed they up the rugged stair, rang their voices out in
  prayer,
Then with England's fatal cord around them cast,
Close beside the gallows tree kissed like brothers lovingly,
True to home and faith and freedom to the last.

Chorus

Never till the latest day shall the memory pass away,
Of the gallant lives thus given for our land;
But on the cause must go, amidst joy and weal and woe,
Till we make our Isle a nation free and grand.

Chorus

On Behalf of Some Irishmen Not Followers of Tradition

George Russell (AE)

George Russell's worthy but vain attempt to correct the balance of Pearse's mythologising of the country, Ireland.

They call us aliens, we are told,
Because our wayward visions stray
From that dim banner they unfold,
The dreams of worn-out yesterday.
The sum of all the past is theirs,
The creeds, the deeds, the fame, the name,
Whose death-created glory flares
And dims the spark of living flame.
They weave the necromancer's spell,
And burst the graves where martyrs slept,
Their ancient story to retell,
Renewing tears the dead have wept.
And they would have us join their dirge,
This worship of an extinct fire
In which they drift beyond the verge
Where races all outworn expire.
The worship of the dead is not
A worship that our hearts allow,
Though every famous shade were wrought
With woven thorns above the brow.
We fling our answer back in scorn:
'We are less children of this clime
Then of some nation yet unborn
Or empire in the womb of time.
We hold the Ireland in the heart
More than the land our eyes have seen,
And love the goal for which we start
More than the tale of what has been.'

The generations as they rise
May live the life men lived before,
Still hold the thought once held as wise,
Go in and out by the same door.
We leave the easy peace it brings:
The few we are shall still unite
In fealty to unseen kings
Or unimaginable light.
We would no Irish sign efface,
But yet our lips would gladlier hail
The firstborn of the Coming Race
Than the last splendour of the Gael.
No blazoned banner we unfold—
One charge alone we give to youth,
Against the sceptred myth to hold
The golden heresy of truth.

I Am Ireland

Patrick Pearse

Pearse's translation of his own poem, "Mise Eire", which contains in microcosm his philosophy of sanguine nationalism.

I am Ireland:
I am older than the Old Woman of Beare.

Great my glory:
I that bore Cuchulainn the valiant.

Great my shame:
My own children that sold their mother.

I am Ireland:
I am lonelier than the Old Woman of Beare.

Renunciation

Patrick Pearse

Pearse's willingness to suffer the blood sacrifice produced some of his most effective poetry. This was written first in Irish and translated into more effective English by himself.

Naked I saw thee,
O beauty of beauty,
And I blinded my eyes
For fear I should fail.

I heard thy music,
O melody of melody,
And I closed my ears
For fear I should falter.

I tasted thy mouth,
O sweetness of sweetness,
And I hardened my heart
For fear of my slaying.

I blinded my eyes,
And I closed my ears,
I hardened my heart
And I smothered my desire.

I turned my back
On the vision I had shaped,
And to this road before me
I turned my face.

I have turned my face
To this road before me,
To the deed that I see
And the death I shall die.

III

The Pleasant Land of Erin

County Mayo

Anthony Raftery

Translated by Frank O'Connor

Raftery's *Cill Aodhain* done into English by Frank O'Connor
with not much loss of the sprightliness of Gaelic's finest spring
song.

Now with the springtime the days will grow longer
    And after St. Bride's Day my sail I'll let go;
I put my mind to it and I never will linger
    Till I find myself back in the County Mayo;
It is in Claremorris I'll stop the first evening
    And at Balla beneath it I'll first take the floor,
I'll go to Kiltimagh and have a month's peace there,
    And that's not two miles from Ballinamore.

I give you my word that the heart in me rises
    As when the wind rises and all the mists go,
Thinking of Carra and Gallen beneath it,
    Scahaveela and all the wide plains of Mayo;
Killeadan's the village where everything pleases,
    Of berries and all sorts of fruit there's no lack,
And if I could but stand in the heart of my people
    Old age would drop from me and youth would come
        back.

The Meeting of the Waters

Thomas Moore

One of the most famous of the *Melodies* and the source of
Leopold Bloom's cloacal musings inspired by the juxtaposi-
tion of Moore's statue by the College Green lavatories. The
site is eagerly sought by visiting tourists who are invariably
disappointed.

There is not in the wide world a valley so sweet,
As the vale in whose bosom the bright waters meet;
Oh! the last rays of feeling and life must depart,
Ere, the bloom of that valley shall fade from my heart,
Ere, the bloom of that valley shall fade from my heart.

Yet it was not that Nature had shed o'er the scene
Her purest of crystal and brightest of green;
'Twas not her soft magic of streamlet or rill,
Oh! no, it was something more exquisite still,
Oh! no, it was something more exquisite still.

'Twas that friends, the belov'd of my bosom, were near,
Who made every dear scene of enchantment more dear;
And who felt how the best charms of nature improve,
When we see them reflected from looks that we love,
When we see them reflected from looks that we love.

Sweet vale of Avoca, how calm could I rest
In thy bosom of shade with the friends I love best,
Where the storms that we feel in this cold world should cease,
And our hearts, like thy waters, be mingled in peace,
And our hearts, like thy waters, be mingled in peace.

Biddy Mulligan
The Pride of the Coombe

Seamus Kavanagh

One of the best known of Dublin songs made famous by
Jimmy O'Dea but sung by others and predating his many
theatre performances as the eponymous heroine.

I'm a buxom fine widow, I live in a spot,
In Dublin they call it the Coombe;
My shops and my stalls are laid out on the street,
And my palace consists of one room.
I sell apples and oranges, nuts and split peas,
Bananas and sugar-stick sweet,
On Saturday night I sell second-hand clothes
From the floor of my stall on the street.

Chorus
You may travel from Clare
To the County Kildare,
From Francis Street on to Macroom,
But where would you see
A fine widow like me?
Biddy Mulligan, the pride of the Coombe.

I sell fish on a Friday, spread out on a board
The finest you'd find in the sae,
But the best is my herrings, fine Dublin Bay herrings,
There's herrings for dinner to-day.
I have a son Mick, and he's great on the flute
He plays in the Longford Street Band,
It would do your heart good to see him march out,
On a Sunday for Dollymount strand.

Chorus

In the Park on a Sunday, I make quite a dash,
The neighbours look on with surprise,
With my Aberdeen shawlie thrown over my head,
I dazzle the sight of their eyes.
At Patrick Street corner for sixty-four years,
I've stood and no one can deny,
That while I stood there, no person could dare
To say black was the white of my eye.

Chorus

Cockles and Mussels

Anonymous

The one Dublin song that has been exported successfully. A
version of the third stanza "She died of the faver/and no one
could save her" is probably older and truer to the accent.
Mollie is buried, perhaps, in St. Audeon's churchyard.

In Dublin's fair city,
Where the girls are so pretty,
    I first set my eyes on sweet Mollie Malone.
She wheeled her wheelbarrow
Through streets broad and narrow,
    Crying, "Cockles and mussels, alive, alive, oh!
      Alive, alive, oh!
      Alive, alive, oh!"
Crying, "Cockles and mussels, alive, alive, oh!"

She was a fishmonger,
But sure 'twas no wonder,
    For so were her father and mother before.
And they both wheeled their barrow
Through streets broad and narrow,
    Crying, "Cockles and mussels, alive, alive, oh!
      Alive, alive, oh!" *etc.*

She died of a fever,
And none could relieve her,
    And that was the end of sweet Mollie Malone.
But her ghost wheels her barrow,
Through streets broad and narrow,
    Crying, "Cockles and mussels, alive, alive, oh!
      Alive, alive, oh!" *etc.*

Dicey Reilly

Anonymous

One of several national songs of the independent republic near Ireland that Dublin in fact is. Not fully understood by ex-urbanites, it is learned and vigorously sung by "culchies" newly come to the Smoke in a vain attempt to establish their metropolitan credentials.

Ah poor oul Dicey Reilly, she has taken to the sup,
And poor oul Dicey Reilly she will never give it up,
It's off each morning to the pop that she goes in for another
     little drop,
But the heart of the rowl is Dicey Reilly.

She will walk along Fitzgibbon Street with an independent
     air
And then it's down by Summerhill, and as the people stare
She'll say "It's nearly half past one, time I went in for
     another little one."
But the heart of the rowl is Dicey Reilly.

Now at two, pubs close and out she goes as happy as a lark
She'll find a bench to sleep it off down in St Patrick's Park.
She'll wake at five feeling in the pink and say "'Tis time for
     another drink."
But the heart of the rowl is Dicey Reilly.

Now she'll travel far to a dockside bar to have another
     round
And after one or two or three she doesn't feel quite sound
And after four she's a bit unstable, after five underneath the
     table
The heart of the rowl is Dicey Reilly.

Oh they carry her home at twelve o'clock as they do every
    night
Bring her inside, put her on the bed and then turn out the
    light.
Next morning she'll get out of bed and look for a curer for
    her head
But the heart of the rowl is Dicey Reilly.

Ah poor oul Dicey Reilly she has taken to the sup
And poor oul Dicey Reilly she will never give it up.
It's off each morning to the pop then she goes in for
    another little drop
But the heart of the rowl is Dicey Reilly.

Waxies Dargle

Anonymous

As with Dicey Reilly, only earlier and more so.

Says my aul' one to your aul' one
Will yeh come to the Waxies Dargle
Says your aul' one to my aul' one
Shure I haven't got a farthin'
I've just been down to Monto Town
To see young Kill McArdle
But he wouldn't lend me half a crown
To go to the Waxies Dargle

Chorus
What are you havin'
Will you have a pint
Yes I'll have a pint
With you sir
And if one of ye doesn't order soon
We'll be thrown out of the boozer

Says my aul' one to your aul' one
Will you come to the Galway Races
Says your aul' one to my aul' one
With the price of my aul' lad's braces
I went down to Capel Street
To the Jew man money lenders
But they wouldn't give me a
couple of bob on
My aul' lad's red suspenders

Chorus

Says my aul' one to your aul' one
We have no beef or mutton
But if we go down to Monto Town
We might get a drink for nuttin
Here's a piece of advice
I got from an aul' fishmonger
When food is scarce
And you see the hearse
You'll know you have died of hunger

Chorus

The Bells of Shandon

Francis Mahony ("Father Prout")

An unsentimental song turned to sentimental use by many
Cork exiles who think it grander than the *Banks*. The teasing
parodic elements are missed or ignored by modern singers.

With deep affection and recollection,
I often think of the Shandon bells,
Whose sounds so wild would, in days of childhood,
Fling round my cradle their magic spells.
And this I ponder, where'er I wander,
And thus grow fonder, sweet Cork, of thee;
With thy bells of Shandon,
That sound so grand on
The pleasant waters of the river Lee.

I have heard bells chiming full many a clime in,
Tolling sublime in Cathedral shrine;
While at a glib rate brass tongues would vibrate,
But all their music spoke naught to thine;
For memory dwelling on each proud swelling,
Of thy belfry knelling its bold notes free,
Made the bells of Shandon,
Sound far more grand on
The pleasant waters of the river Lee.

I have heard bells tolling, "Old Adrian's Mole" in,
Their thunder rolling from the Vatican,
With cymbals glorious, swinging uproarious,
In the gorgeous turrets of Notre Dame;
But thy sounds were sweeter than the dome of Peter,
Flings o'er the Tiber, pealing solemnly,
Oh! the bells of Shandon,
Sound far more grand on
The pleasant waters of the river Lee.

There's a bell in Moscow, while on tower and Kiosko,
In St. Sophia the Turkman gets,
And loud in air calls men to prayer,
From the tapering summit of tall minarets.
Such empty phantom I freely grant them,
But there's an anthem more dear to me,
It's the bells of Shandon,
That sound so grand on
The pleasant waters of the river Lee.

Dawn on the Irish Coast

John Locke

Sometimes known as the exile's anthem, this poem is often quoted by literate Americans to the confusion and embarrassment of their hosts.

T'anam chun Dia! there it is—
   The dawn on the hills of Ireland,
God's Angels lifting the night's black veil
   From the fair sweet face of my sireland!
O! Ireland, isn't it grand you look—
   Like a bride in her rich adornin!
With all the pent-up love of my heart,
   I bid you the top of the mornin'!

This one short hour pays lavish back,
   For many a year of mourning;
I'd almost venture another flight,
   There's so much joy in returning—
Watching out for the hallowed shore,
   All other attractions scornin';
O, Ireland! don't you hear me shout?
   I bid you the top of the mornin'!

Ho, ho, upon Cliodhna's shelving strand,
   The surges are grandly heaving,
And Kerry is pushing her headlands out,
   To give us the kindly greeting!
Into the shore the sea-birds fly,
   On pinions that know no drooping,
And out on the cliffs, with welcome charged,
   A million of waves come trooping.

Oh, kindly, generous Irish land,
  So leal and fair and loving!
No wonder the wandering Celt should think
  And dream of you in his roving.
The alien home may have gems and gold,
  Shadows may never have gloomed it;
But the heart will sigh for the absent land
  Where the lovelight first illumed it.

And doesn't old Cove look charming there,
  Watching the wild waves' motion,
Leaning her back up against the hills,
  And the tip of her toes in the ocean.
I wonder I don't hear Shandon's bells—
  Ah! maybe their chiming's over,
For it's many a year since I began
  The life of a Western rover.

For thirty summers, a stoir mo chroidhe,
  Those hills I now feast my eyes on
Ne'er met my vision save when they rose
  Over memory's dim horizon.
E'en so 'twas grand and fair they seemed
  In the landscape spread before me;
But dreams are dreams, and my eyes would ope',
  To see Texas's skies still o'er me.

Oh! often upon the Texas plains,
  When the day and the chase were over,
My thoughts would fly o'er the weary wave,
  And around the coast-line hover;
And the prayer would rise that some future day—
  All danger and doubting scorning—
I'd help to win for my native land,
  The light of young liberty's morning!

Now fuller and truer the shore-line shows;
  Was ever a scene so splendid?

I feel the breath of the Munster breeze,
   Thank God that my exile's ended!
Old scenes, old songs, old friends again,
   The vale and the cot I was born in—
O, Ireland, up from my heart of hearts,
   I bid you the top of the mornin'!

The Spanish Lady

Joseph Campbell

The oldest and most swingeing version of a song that tends towards too much refinement as a concert piece. Joseph Campbell's work as collector and editor of songs is more important than his own poetry.

As I walked down through Dublin City
At the hour of twelve in the night
Who should I spy but a Spanish Lady
Washing her feet by candlelight?
First she dipped them, then she dried them
Over a fire of ambery coal.
Never in all my life did I see
A maid so neat about the sole.

I stopped to peep, but the Watchman passed
And says: young fellow, the night is late
Get home to bed or I'll wrastle you
At a double trot through the Bridewell Gate!
So I waved a kiss to the Spanish Lady
Hot as the fire of cramesy coal
I've seen dark maids, though never one
So white and neat about the sole.

O, she's too rich for a Poddle swaddy
With her tortoise comb and mantle fine,
A Hellfire buck would fit her better,
Drinking brandy and claret wine.
I'm just a decent College sizar,
Poor as a sod of smouldery coal;
And how would I dress the Spanish Lady
And she so neat about the sole?

O, she'd make a mott for the Provost Marshal
Or a wife for the Mayor on his coach so high,
Or a queen for Andalusia
Kicking her heel in the Cardinal's eye.
I'm blue as cockles, brown as herrings
Over a grid of glimmery coal
And all because of the Spanish Lady
So mortial neat about the sole.

I wandered north, and I wandered south
By Golden Lane and Patrick's Close,
The Coombe, Smithfield and Stoneybatter,
Back to Napper Tandy's house.
Old age has laid its hand upon me
Cold as a fire of ashy coal
And where is the lovely Spanish Lady
That maid so neat about the sole?

On the Banks of My Own Lovely Lee

Jonathan C. Hanrahan

The true anthem of doomed Corkmen (not the suspect "Bell of Shandon"). It is the theme of many mild anti-second-city jokes.

How oft do my thoughts in their fancy take flight,
To the home of my childhood away.
To the days when each Patriot's vision seem'd bright,
'Ere I dream'd that those joys should decay.
When my heart was as light as the wild winds that blow,
Down the Mardyke through each elm tree.
Where I sported and played 'neath each green leafy shade,
On the banks of my own lovely Lee.
Where I sported and played 'neath each green leafy shade,
On the banks of my own lovely Lee.

And then in the springtime of laughter and song,
Can I ever forget the sweet hours.
With the friends of my youth, as we rambled along,
'Mongst the green mossy banks and wild flowers.
Then, too, when the evening sun sinking to rest
Sheds its golden light over the sea,
The maid with her lover the wild daisies press'd,
On the banks of my own lovely Lee.
The maid with her lover the wild daisies press'd
On the banks of my own lovely Lee.

'Tis a beautiful land this dear Isle of song
Its gems shed their light on the world,
And her faithful sons bore thro' ages of wrong
The standard St. Patrick unfurled.
Oh! would I were there with the friends I love best,
And my fond bosom's partner with me
We'd roam thy banks over, and when weary we'd rest
By thy waters, my own lovely Lee.

Oh, what joys should be mine 'ere this life should decline
To seek shells on thy sea-girdled shore,
While the steel-feathered eagle, oft splashing the brine,
Brings longing for freedom once more.
Oh, all that on earth I wish for or crave
Is that my last crimson drop be for thee,
To moisten the grass of my fore-fathers' grave
On the banks of my own lovely Lee.

Going Home

Patrick MacGill

A rare mood of lyricism that is generally hidden in MacGill's
novel, *Children of the Dead End*, is seen here in his tribute to
his native place. It has been set to music, and the alchemic
combination of words and music produces a very moving
piece.

I'm going back to Glenties when the harvest fields are
          brown,
And the Autumn sunset lingers on my little Irish town,
    When the gossamer is shining where the moorland
          blossoms blow
    I'll take the road across the hills I tramped so long ago—
'Tis far I am beyond the seas, but yearning voices call,
"Will you not come back to Glenties, and your wave-
          washed Donegal?"

I've seen the hopes of childhood stifled by the hand of
          time,
I've seen the smile of innocence become the frown of crime.
    I've seen the wrong rise high and strong, I've seen the
          fair betrayed,
    Until the faltering heart fell low the brave became
          afraid—
But still the cry comes out to me, the homely voices call,
From the Glen among the highlands of my ancient
          Donegal.

Sure, I think I see them often, when the night steals o'er the
          town,
The Braes of old Strasala, and the homes of Carrigdoun—

There's a light in Jimmy Lynch's house, a shadow on the
  blind.
I often watched the shadow, for 'twas Mary in behind.
And often in the darkness, 'tis myself that sees it all,
For I cannot help but dreaming of the folk in Donegal.

So I'll hie me back to Glenties when the harvest comes
  again,
And the kine are in the pasture and the berries in the lane,
  Then they'll give me such a welcome that my heart will
    leap for joy,
  When my father and my mother welcome back their
    wayward boy.
So I'm going back to Glenties when the autumn showers
  fall,
And the harvest home is cheery in my dear old Donegal.

Galway

Mary Davenport O'Neill

A poem which superficially is no longer applicable to the showpiece of Ireland's industrialisation but is still quite true about the basic Galwegian temper.

I know a town tormented by the sea,
And there time goes slow
That the people see it flow
And watch it drowsily,
And growing older hour by hour they say,
"Please God, to-morrow!
Then we will work and play,"
And their tall houses crumble away.
This town is eaten through with memory
Of pride and thick red Spanish wine and gold
And a great come and go;
But the sea is cold,
And the spare, black trees
Crouch in the withering breeze
That blows from the sea,
And the land stands bare and alone,
For its warmth is turned away
And its strength held in hard cold grey-blue stone;
And the people are heard to say,
Through the raving of the jealous sea,
"Please God, to-morrow!
Then we will work and play."

At Oranmore

Anonymous

A typical "encounter" song in the "As I roved out" tradition.
Decent Irish reticence draws a veil over what happened
between the second-last and last verses.

At Oranmore in the County Galway,
   One pleasant evening in the month of May,
I spied a damsel, she was young and handsome—
   Her beauty fairly took my breath away.

Chorus
She wore no jewels, nor costly diamonds,
   No paint or powder, no, none at all.
But she wore a bonnet with the shamrock on it,
   And round her shoulder was a Galway shawl.

We kept on walking, she kept on talking,
   'Till her father's cottage came into view.
Says she: "Come in, sir, and meet my father,
   And play to please him 'The Foggy Dew'."

She sat me down beside the hearthstone,
   I could see her father, he was six feet tall.
And soon her mother had the kettle singing—
   All I could think of was the Galway shawl.

Chorus

I played "The Blackbird," and "The Stack of Barley,"
   "Rodney's Glory" and "The Foggy Dew,"
She sang each note like an Irish linnet,
   Whilst the tears stood in her eyes of blue.

'Twas early, early, all in the morning,
   When I hit the road for old Donegal.
She said: "Goodbye, sir," she cried and kissed me,
   And my heart remained with that Galway shawl.

Chorus

The Ould Lammas Fair

Anonymous

The Lammas Fair takes place in Ballycastle, County Antrim, on the 31st August each year. Dulse and yellow-man (a virulent, anti-dental home-made toffee) are still sold.

At the Ould Lammas Fair in Ballycastle long ago,
I met a little colleen, who set my heart a-glow;
She was smiling at her daddy buying lambs from Paddy
     Roe
At the Ould Lammas Fair in Ballycastle O!

Chorus
At the Ould Lammas Fair, boys, were you ever there.
   Were you ever at the fair in Ballycastle O?
Did you treat your Mary Ann to dulse and yellow man
   At the Ould Lammas Fair at Ballycastle O?

In Flanders fields afar while resting from the war,
We drank Bon-Sante to the Flemish lassies O;
But the scene that haunts my memory is kissing Mary Ann,
Her pouting lips all sticky from eating yellow man.
As we crossed the silver Margey and strolled across the
     strand,
From the Ould Lammas Fair at Ballycastle O!

There's a neat little cabin on the slopes of ould Knocklade
It's lit by love and sunshine where the heather honey's
     made.
By the bees ever humming and our childer's joyous call,
Resounds across the valley when the shadows fall.
I take my fiddle down and my Mary smiling there
Brings back a happy memory of the Ould Lammas Fair.

I'll Tell My Ma

Anonymous

A child's skipping song of great adaptability since it can with
little change be applied to any of Ireland's "cities".

I'll tell my ma when I go home,
The boys won't leave the girls alone,
They pull my hair, they stole my comb.
But that's all right 'till I go home.
She is handsome, she is pretty,
She is the belle of Belfast City,
She is courtin' one, two, three,
Please won't you tell me who is she?

Albert Mooney says he loves her,
All the boys are fighting for her,
They rap at the door, and they ring the bell,
Saying O my true love are you well?
Out she comes as white as snow,
Rings on her fingers, bells on her toes,
Old Johnny Murray says she'll die,
If she doesn't get the fellow with the roving eye.

Ulster Names

John Hewitt

One of the finest topographical poems ever written, by one of
Ireland's finest poets. When all comes to all, local patriotism
breaks fewest heads.

I take my stand by the Ulster names,
each clean hard name like a weathered stone;
Tyrella, Rostrevor, are flickering flames:
The names I mean are The Moy, Malone,
Strabane, Slieve Gullion and Portglenone.

Even suppose that each name were freed
from legend's ivy and history's moss,
there'd be music still, in say, Carrick-a-rede,
though men forget it's the rock across
the track of the salmon from Islay and Ross.

The names of a land shew the heart of the race;
they move on the tongue like the lilt of a song.
You say the name and I see the place—
Drumbo, Dungannon, or Annalong.
Barony, townland, we cannot go wrong.

You say Armagh, and I see the hill
with the two tall spires or the square low tower;
the faith of Patrick is with us still;
his blessing falls in a moonlit hour,
when the apple-orchards are all in flower.

You whisper Derry. Beyond the walls
and the crashing boom and the coiling smoke,
I follow that freedom which beckons and calls

to Colmcille tall in his grove of oak
raising his voice for the rhyming folk.

County by county you number them over;
Tyrone, Fermanagh. . . I stand by a lake,
and the bubbling curlew, the whistling plover
call over the whins in the chill day-break
as the hills and the waters the first light take.

Let Down be famous for care-tilled earth,
for the little green hills and the harsh grey peaks,
the rocky bed of the Lagan's birth,
the white farm fat in the August weeks.
There's one more county my pride still seeks.

You give it the name and my quick thoughts run
through the narrow towns with their wheels of trade,
to Glenballyemon, Glenaan, Glendun,
from Trostan down to the braes of Layde
for there is the place where the pact was made.

But you have as good a right as I
to praise the place where your face is known,
for over us all is the selfsame sky;
the limestone's locked in the strength of the bone,
and who shall mock at the steadfast stone?

So it's Ballinamallard, it's Crossmaglen,
It's Aughnacloy, it's Donaghadee,
It's Magherafelt breeds the best of men
I'll not deny it. But look for me
on the moss between Orra and Slievenanee.

Dublin Made Me

Donagh MacDonagh

A fine blast of a trumpet against the monstrous regiments of red-necks by one whose moral frontiers were Finglas and Lucan. Unfair, polemical and entirely admirable.

Dublin made me and no little town
With the country closing in on its streets
The cattle walking proudly on its pavements
The jobbers, the gombeenmen and the cheats

Devouring the fair-day between them
A public-house to half a hundred men
And the teacher, the solicitor and the bank-clerk
In the hotel bar drinking for ten.

Dublin made me, not the secret poteen still
The raw and hungry hills of the West
The lean road flung over profitless bog
Where only a snipe could nest

Where the sea takes its tithe of every boat,
Bawneen and currach have no allegiance of mine,
Nor the cute self-deceiving talkers of the South
Who look to the East for a sign.

The soft and dreary midlands with their tame canals
Wallow between sea and sea, remote from adventure,
And Northward a far and fortified province
Crouches under the lash of arid censure.

I disclaim all fertile meadows, all tilled land
The evil that grows from it and the good,
But the Dublin of old statutes, this arrogant city,
Stirs proudly and secretly in my blood.

IV
The Next Market Day

The Low-Backed Car

Samuel Lover

Lover's most famous song, used by him as part of the theatrical entertainment which he called *An Irish Evening* and with which he toured, anticipating Percy French. The mock-heroic elements in verse two mark it as early Victorian.

When first I saw sweet Peggy,
'Twas on a market day,
A low-backed car she drove, and sat
Upon a truss of hay;
But when that hay was blooming grass,
And decked with flowers of spring,
No flow'r was there that could compare
With the blooming girl I sing.

Chorus
As she sat in the low-backed car,
The man at the turnpike bar
Never asked for a toll,
But just rubbed his owld poll
And looked after the low-backed car.

In battle's wild commotion,
The proud and mighty Mars,
With hostile scythes, demands his tithes
Of death—in warlike cars.
While Peggy, peaceful goddess
Has darts in her bright eye,
That knock men down, in the market town
As right and left they fly—
While she sits in her low-backed car,
Than battle more dangerous far—
For the doctor's art
Cannot cure the heart
That is hit from that low-backed car.

Sweet Peggy, round her car, sir,
Has strings of ducks and geese,
But the scores of hearts she slaughters
By far out-number these;
While she among her poultry sits
Just like a turtle dove,
Well-worth the cage, I do engage,
Of the blooming god of love!

While she sits in her low-backed car,
The lovers came near and far,
And envy the chicken
That Peggy is pickin',
As she sits in the low-backed car.

O, I'd rather own that car, sir
With Peggy by me side,
Than a coach-and-four and gold galore,
And a lady for my bride;
For the lady would sit forninst me
On a cushion made with taste,
While Peggy would sit beside me
With my arm around her waist—
While we drove in the low-backed car,
To be married by Father Maher,
Oh, my heart would beat high,
At her glance and her sigh
Though it beat in a low-backed car.

The Next Market Day

Anonymous

Herbert Hughes, an Ulsterman, found this song and in his musical arrangement of it applied it to the Strangford Lough town of Comber (pronounced to rhyme with "sombre") though earlier versions named Sligo and other Irish towns. It is one of the liveliest of the "encounter" *genre*.

A maid goin' to Comber, her markets to larn,
To sell for her mammy three hanks o' fine yarn,
She met with a young man along the highway,
Which caused this young damsel to dally and stray.

Chorus
Sit ye beside me, I mean ye no harm,
Sit ye beside me this new tune to larn,
Here is three guineas your mammy to pay,
So lay by your yarn till the next market day.

They sat down together, the grass it was green,
And the day was the fairest that ever was seen,
Oh, the look in your eye beats a mornin' o' May,
I could sit by your side till the next market day.

Chorus

This young maid went home and the words that he said
And the air that he played her still rang in her head;
She says I'll go find him by land or by sea,
Till he larns me that tune called The Next Market Day.

Four Ducks on a Pond

William Allingham

Allingham's epiphany of youthful innocence remembered by a man notoriously soft and easily dismayed by the more brutal aspects of life in his homeland.

Four ducks on a pond,
A grass-bank beyond,
A blue sky of spring,
White birds on the wing:
What a little thing
To remember for years—
To remember with tears!

The Stone Outside Dan Murphy's Door

Johnny Patterson

One of Johnny Patterson's famous circus songs. After traditional clowning in classical make-up he would sing (a purely Irish practice this) one of his own very popular songs. Clare people claim to be able to point out the actual stone in Patterson's native county, but then Clare people will claim anything.

There's a sweet garden spot in our mem'ry,
It's the place we were born and reared;
'Tis long years ago since we left it,
But return there we will if we're spared.
Our friends and companions of childhood
Would assemble each night near a score,
'Round Dan Murphy's shop and how often we've sat
On the stone that stood outside his door!

Chorus
Those days in our hearts we will cherish,
Contented, although we were poor,
And the songs that were sung in the days we were young,
On the stone outside Dan Murphy's door!

When our day's work was over we'd meet there
In the winter or spring the same.
The boys and the girls all together,
Then would join in some innocent game,
Dan Murphy would bring down his fiddle,
While his daughter looked after the store,
The music did ring and sweet songs we would sing
On the stone outside Dan Murphy's door!

Chorus

Back again will our thoughts often wander,
To the scenes of our childhood's home,
The friends and companions we left there
It was poverty caused us to roam.
Since then in this life we have prospered,
But now still in our hearts we feel sore
For mem'ry will fly to the days now gone by,
And the stone outside Dan Murphy's door!

Chorus

The Donovans

Francis A. Fahy

Written from lifelong exile in London, this is one of Frank
Fahy's great songs. *Cannawaun* is bog-cotton and, in case
there may be anyone who does not know it, *caubeen* is hat.

If you would like to see the height of hospitality,
The cream of kindly welcome, and the core of cordiality:
Joys of all the olden time—you're wishing to recall again?
Come down to Donovans, and there you'll meet them all
    again.

Céad míle fáilte they'll give you down at Donovans,
As cheery as the springtime and Irish as the *cannawaun*
The wish of my heart is, if ever I had any one—
That every luck that lightens life may light upon the
    Donovans.

As soon as e'er you lift the latch, the little ones are meeting
    you;
Soon as you're beneath the thatch, oh! kindly looks are
    greeting you:
Scarcely are you ready to be holding out the fist to them,
When down by the fireside you're sitting in the midst of
    them.
Céad míle fáilte they'll give you down at Donovans,
    etc.

There sits the *cailín deas*—oh! where on earth's the peer of
    her?
The modest face, the gentle grace, the humor and the cheer
    of her—

Eyes like the summer skies when twin stars beam above in
　　them,
Oh! proud will be the boy that's to light the lamp of love in
　　them.
Céad míle fáilte they'll give you down at Donovans,
　　etc.

Then when you rise to go, it's "Ah, then, now sit down
　　again!"
"Isn't it the haste you're in?" and "Won't you soon come
　　round again?"
Your *caubeen* and your overcoat you'd better put astray
　　from them,
'Twill take you all your time to try and tear yourself away
　　from them.
Céad míle fáilte they'll give you down at Donovans,
　　etc.

Danny

John Millington Synge

The other side of Irish country life and one greatly relished by
the wilder spirit of Synge.

One night a score of Erris men,
A score I'm told and nine,
Said, "We'll get shut of Danny's noise
Of girls and widows dyin'.

"There's not his like from Binghamstown
To Boyle and Ballycroy,
At playing hell on decent girls,
At beating man and boy.

"He's left two pairs of female twins
Beyond in Killacreest,
And twice in Crossmolina fair
He's struck the parish priest.

"But we'll come round him in the night
A mile beyond the Mullet;
Ten will quench his bloody eyes,
And ten will choke his gullet."

It wasn't long till Danny came,
From Bangor making way,
And he was damning moon and stars
And whistling grand and gay.

Till in a gap of hazel glen—
And not a hare in sight—
Out lepped the nine-and-twenty lads
Along his left and right.

Then Danny smashed the nose on Byrne,
He split the lips on three,
and bit across the right-hand thumb
Of one Red Shawn Magee.

But seven tripped him up behind,
And seven kicked before,
And seven squeezed around his throat
Till Danny kicked no more.

Then some destroyed him with their heels,
Some tramped him in the mud,
Some stole his purse and timber pipe,
And some washed off his blood.

And when you're walking out the way
From Bangor to Belmullet,
You'll see a flat cross on a stone,
Where men choked Danny's gullet.

Riders to the Sea

John Millington Synge

Possibly the finest short play ever written, dignified, beautiful and in its tempo possessing something of the slow swell of the sea.

PERSONS IN THE PLAY

> MAURYA, an old woman
> BARTLEY, her son
> CATHLEEN, her daughter
> NORA, a younger daughter
> MEN AND WOMEN

Scene: an Island off the West of Ireland

Cottage kitchen, with nets, oilskins, spinning-wheel, some new boards standing by the wall, etc. Cathleen, a girl of about twenty, finishes kneading cake, and puts it down in the pot-oven by the fire; then wipes her hands, and begins to spin at the wheel. Nora, a young girl, puts her head in at the door.

NORA *in a low voice:* Where is she?
CATHLEEN: She's lying down, God help her, and maybe sleeping, if she's able.

Nora comes in softly, and takes a bundle from under her shawl.

Spinning the wheel rapidly. What is it you have?

NORA: The young priest is after bringing them. It's a shirt and a plain stocking were got off a drowned man in Donegal.

Cathleen stops her wheel with a sudden movement, and leans out to listen.

We're to find out if it's Michael's they are, some time herself will be down looking by the sea.

CATHLEEN: How would they be Michael's, Nora? How would he go the length of that way to the far north?

NORA: The young priest says he's known the like of it. "If it's Michael's they are," says he, "you can tell herself he's got a clean burial, by the grace of God; and if they're not his, let no one say a word about them, for she'll be getting her death," says he, "with crying and lamenting."

The door which Nora half closed is blown open by a gust of wind.

CATHLEEN *looking out anxiously:* Did you ask him would he stop Bartley going this day with the horses to the Galway fair?

NORA: "I won't stop him," says he; "but let you not be afraid. Herself does be saying prayers half through the night, and the Almighty God won't leave her destitute," says he, "with no son living."

CATHLEEN: Is the sea bad by the white rocks, Nora?

NORA: Middling bad, God help us. There's a great roaring in the west, and it's worse it'll be getting when the tide's turned to the wind. *She goes over to the table with the bundle.* Shall I open it now?

CATHLEEN: Maybe she'd wake up on us, and come in before we'd done. *Coming to the table.* It's a long time we'll be, and the two of us crying.

NORA *goes to the inner door and listens:* She's moving about on the bed. She'll be coming in a minute.

CATHLEEN: Give me the ladder, and I'll put them up in the turf loft, the way she won't know of them at all, and maybe when the tide turns she'll be going down to see would he be floating from the east.

They put the ladder against the gable of the chimney; Cathleen goes up a few steps and hides the bundle in the turf loft. Maurya comes from the inner room.

MAURYA *looking up at Cathleen and speaking querulously:* Isn't it turf enough you have for this day and evening?

CATHLEEN: There's a cake baking at the fire for a short space (*throwing down the turf*), and Bartley will want it when the tide turns if he goes to Connemara.

Nora picks up the turf and puts it round the pot-oven.

MAURYA *sitting down on a stool at the fire:* He won't go this day with the wind rising from the south and west. He won't go this day, for the young priest will stop him surely.

NORA: He'll not stop him, mother; and I heard Eamon Simon and Stephen Pheety and Colum Shawn saying he would go.

MAURYA: Where is he itself?

NORA: He went down to see would there be another boat sailing in the week, and I'm thinking it won't be long till he's here now, for the tide's turning at the green head, and the hooker's tacking from the east.

CATHLEEN: I hear someone passing the big stones.

NORA *looking out:* He's coming now, and he in a hurry.

BARTLEY *comes in and looks round the room. Speaking sadly and quietly:* Where is the bit of new rope, Cathleen, was bought in Connemara?

CATHLEEN *coming down:* Give it to him, Nora; it's on a nail by the white boards. I hung it up this morning, for the pig with the black feet was eating it.

NORA: *giving him a rope:* Is that it, Bartley?

MAURYA: You'd do right to leave that rope, Bartley, hanging by the boards. *Bartley takes the rope.* It will be wanting

in this place, I'm telling you, if Michael is washed up
to-morrow morning, or the next morning, or any morn-
ing in the week; for it's a deep grave we'll make him, by
the grace of God.

BARTLEY *beginning to work with the rope:* I've no halter the
way I can ride down on the mare, and I must go now
quickly. This is the one boat going for two weeks or
beyond it, and the fair will be a good fair for horses, I
heard them saying below.

MAURYA: It's a hard thing they'll be saying below if the body
is washed up and there's no man in it to make the coffin,
and I after giving a big price for the finest white boards
you'd find in Connemara. *She looks round at the boards.*

BARTLEY: How would it be washed up, and we after looking
each day for nine days, and a strong wind blowing a
while back from the west and south?

MAURYA: If it isn't found itself, that wind is raising the sea,
and there was a star up against the moon, and it rising in
the night. If it was a hundred horses, or a thousand horses
you had itself, what is the price of a thousand horses
against a son where there is one son only?

BARTLEY *working at the halter, to Cathleen:* Let you go down
each day, and see the sheep aren't jumping in on the rye,
and if the jobber comes you can sell the pig with the black
feet if there is a good price going.

MAURYA: How would the like of her get a good price for a
pig?

BARTLEY *to Cathleen:* If the west winds holds with the last bit
of the moon let you and Nora get up weed enough for
another cock for the kelp. It's hard set we'll be from this
day with no one in it but one man to work.

MAURYA: It's hard set we'll be surely the day you're drowned
with the rest. What way will I live and the girls with me,
and I an old woman looking for the grave?

*Bartley lays down the halter, takes off his old coat, and puts on
a newer one of the same flannel.*

BARTLEY *to Nora:* Is she coming to the pier?

NORA *looking out:* She's passing the green head and letting fall her sails.

BARTLEY *getting his purse and tobacco:* I'll have half an hour to go down, and you'll see me coming again in two days, or in three days, or maybe in four days if the wind is bad.

MAURYA *turning round to the fire, and putting her shawl over her head:* Isn't it a hard and cruel man won't hear a word from an old woman, and she holding him from the sea?

CATHLEEN: It's the life of a young man to be going on the sea, and who would listen to an old woman with one thing and she saying it over?

BARTLEY *taking the halter:* I must go now quickly. I'll ride down on the red mare, and the grey pony 'ill run behind me. . . . The blessing of God on you.

He goes out.

MAURYA *crying out as he is in the door:* He's gone now, God spare us, and we'll not see him again. He's gone now, and when the black night is falling I'll have no son left me in the world.

CATHLEEN: Why wouldn't you give him your blessing and he looking round in the door? Isn't it sorrow enough is on every one in this house without your sending him out with an unlucky word behind him, and a hard word in his ear?

Maurya takes up the tongs and begins raking the fire aimlessly without looking round.

NORA *turning towards her:* You're taking away the turf from the cake.

CATHLEEN *crying out:* The Son of God forgive us, Nora, we're after forgetting his bit of bread. *She comes over to the fire.*

NORA: And it's destroyed he'll be going till dark night, and he after eating nothing since the sun went up.

CATHLEEN *turning the cake out of the oven:* It's destroyed he'll be surely. There's no sense left on any person in a house where an old woman will be talking for ever.

Maurya sways herself on her stool.

> *Cutting off some of the bread and rolling it in a cloth; to Maurya.* Let you go down now to the spring well and give him this and he passing. You'll see him then and the dark word will be broken, and you can say "God speed you," the way he'll be easy in his mind.

MAURYA *taking the bread:* Will I be in it as soon as himself?

CATHLEEN: If you go now quickly.

MAURYA *standing up unsteadily:* It's hard set I am to walk.

CATHLEEN *looking at her anxiously:* Give her the stick, Nora, or maybe she'll slip on the big stones.

NORA: What stick?

CATHLEEN: The stick Michael brought from Connemara.

MAURYA *taking a stick Nora gives her:* In the big world the old people do be leaving things after them for their sons and children, but in this place it is the young men do be leaving things behind for them that do be old.

She goes out slowly. Nora goes over to the ladder.

CATHLEEN: Wait, Nora, maybe she'd turn back quickly. She's that sorry, God help her, you wouldn't know the thing she'd do.

NORA: Is she gone round by the bush?

CATHLEEN *looking out:* She's gone now. Throw it down quickly, for the Lord knows when she'll be out of it again.

NORA *getting the bundle from the loft:* The young priest said he'd be passing to-morrow, and we might go down and speak to him below if it's Michael's they are surely.

CATHLEEN *taking the bundle:* Did he say what way they were found?

NORA *coming down:* "There were two men," said he, "and they rowing round with poteen before the cocks crowed, and the oar of one of them caught the body, and they passing the black cliffs of the north."

CATHLEEN *trying to open the bundle:* Give me a knife, Nora; the string's perished with the salt water, and there's a black knot on it you wouldn't loosen in a week.

NORA *giving her a knife:* I've heard tell it was a long way to Donegal.

CATHLEEN *cutting the string:* It is surely. There was a man in here a while ago—the man sold us that knife—and he said if you set off walking from the rocks beyond, it would be in seven days you'd be in Donegal.

NORA: And what time would a man take, and he floating?

Cathleen opens the bundle and takes out a bit of a shirt and a stocking. They look at them eagerly.

CATHLEEN *in a low voice:* The Lord spare us, Nora! isn't it a queer hard thing to say if it's his they are surely?

NORA: I'll get his shirt off the hook the way we can put the one flannel on the other. *She looks through some clothes hanging in the corner.* It's not with them, Cathleen, and where will be it?

CATHLEEN: I'm thinking Bartley put it on him in the morning, for his own shirt was heavy with the salt in it. *Pointing to the corner.* There's a bit of a sleeve was of the same stuff. Give me that and it will do.

Nora brings it to her and they compare the flannel.

It's the same stuff, Nora; but if it is itself, aren't there great rolls of it in the shops of Galway, and isn't it many another man may have a shirt of it as well as Michael himself?

NORA *who has taken up the stocking and counted the stitches, crying out:* It's Michael, Cathleen, it's Michael; God

spare his soul, and what will herself say when she hears
this story, and Bartley on the sea?

CATHLEEN *taking the stocking:* It's a plain stocking.

NORA: It's the second one of the third pair I knitted, and I put
up three-score stitches, and I dropped four of them.

CATHLEEN *counts the stitches:* It's that number is in it. *Crying
out.* Ah, Nora, isn't it a bitter thing to think of him
floating that way to the far north, and no one to keen
him but the black hags that do be flying on the sea?

NORA *swinging herself half round, and throwing out her arms
on the clothes:* And isn't it a pitiful thing when there is
nothing left of a man who was a great rower and fisher
but a bit of an old shirt and a plain stocking?

CATHLEEN *after an instant:* Tell me is herself coming, Nora?
I hear a little sound on the path.

NORA *looking out:* She is, Cathleen. She's coming up to the
door.

CATHLEEN: Put these things away before she'll come in. Maybe
it's easier she'll be after giving her blessing to Bartley, and
we won't let on we've heard anything the time he's on
the sea.

NORA *helping Cathleen to close the bundle:* We'll put them
here in the corner.

*They put them into a hole in the chimney corner. Cathleen
goes back to the spinning-wheel.*

Will she see it was crying I was?

CATHLEEN: Keep your back to the door the way the light'll
not be on you.

*Nora sits down at the chimney corner, with her back to the
door. Maurya comes in very slowly, without looking at the
girls, and goes over to her stool at the other side of the fire. The
cloth with the bread is still in her hand. The girls look at each
other, and Nora points to the bundle of bread.*

After spinning for a moment. You didn't give him his bit of bread?

Maurya begins to keen softly, without turning round.

Did you see him riding down?

Maurya goes on keening.

A little impatiently. God forgive you; isn't it a better thing to raise your voice and tell what you seen, than to be making lamentation for a thing that's done? Did you see Bartley, I'm saying to you?

MAURYA *with a weak voice:* My heart's broken from this day.

CATHLEEN *as before:* Did you see Bartley?

MAURYA: I seen the fearfullest thing.

CATHLEEN *leaves her wheel and looks out:* God forgive you; he's riding the mare now over the green head, and the grey pony behind him.

MAURYA *starts so that her shawl falls back from her head and shows her white tossed hair. With a frightened voice:* The grey pony behind him. . . .

CATHLEEN *coming to the fire:* What is it ails you at all?

MAURYA *speaking very slowly:* I've seen the fearfullest thing any person has seen since the day Bride Dara seen the dead man with the child in his arms.

CATHLEEN *and* NORA: Uah.

They crouch down in front of the old woman at the fire.

NORA: Tell us what it is you seen.

MAURYA: I went down to the spring well, and I stood there saying a prayer to myself. Then Bartley came along, and he riding on the red mare with the grey pony behind him. *She puts up her hands, as if to hide something from her eyes.* The Son of God spare us, Nora!

CATHLEEN: What is it you seen?

MAURYA: I seen Michael himself.

CATHLEEN *speaking softly:* You did not, mother. It wasn't
  Michael you seen, for his body is after being found in the
  far north, and he's got a clean burial, by the grace of
  God.

MAURYA *a little defiantly:* I'm after seeing him this day, and he
  riding and galloping. Bartley came first on the red mare,
  and I tried to say "God speed you," but something
  choked the words in my throat. He went by quickly; and
  "The blessing of God on you," says he, and I could say
  nothing. I looked up then, and I crying, at the grey pony,
  and there was Michael upon it—with fine clothes on him,
  and new shoes on his feet.

CATHLEEN *begins to keen:* It's destroyed we are from this day.
  It's destroyed, surely.

NORA: Didn't the young priest say the Almighty God won't
  leave her destitute with no son living?

MAURYA *in a low voice, but clearly:* It's little the like of him
  knows of the sea. . . . Bartley will be lost now, and let
  you call in Eamon and make me a good coffin out of the
  white boards, for I won't live after them. I've had a
  husband, and a husband's father, and six sons in this
  house—six fine men, though it was a hard birth I had
  with every one of them and they coming into the world—
  and some of them were found and some of them were
  not found, but they're gone now the lot of them. . . .
  There were Stephen and Shawn were lost in the great
  wind, and found after in the Bay of Gregory of the
  Golden Mouth, and carried up the two of them on one
  plank, and in by that door.

*She pauses for a moment; the girls start as if they heard
something through the door that is half open behind them.*

NORA *in a whisper:* Did you hear that, Cathleen? Did you
  hear a noise in the north-east?

CATHLEEN *in a whisper:* There's someone after crying out by
  the seashore.

MAURYA *continues without hearing anything:* There was Shea-mus and his father, and his own father again, were lost in a dark night, and not a stick or sign was seen of them when the sun went up. There was Patch after was drowned out of a curragh that turned over. I was sitting here with Bartley, and he a baby, lying on my two knees, and I seen two women, and three women, and four women coming in, and they crossing themselves and not saying a word. I looked out then, and there were men coming after them, and they holding a thing in the half of a red sail, and water dripping out of it—it was a dry day, Nora—and leaving a track to the door.

She pauses again with her hand stretched out towards the door. It opens softly and old women begin to come in, crossing themselves on the threshold, and kneeling down in front of the stage with red petticoats over their heads.

Half in a dream, to Cathleen. Is it Patch, or Michael, or what is it at all?

CATHLEEN: Michael is after being found in the far north, and when he is found there how could he be here in this place?

MAURYA: There does be a power of young men floating round in the sea, and what way would they know if it was Michael they had, or another man like him, for when a man is nine days in the sea, and the wind blowing, it's hard set his own mother would be to say what man was in it.

CATHLEEN: It's Michael, God spare him, for they're after sending us a bit of his clothes from the far north.

She reaches out and hands Maurya the clothes that belonged to Michael. Maurya stands up slowly, and takes them in her hands. Nora looks out.

NORA: They're carrying a thing among them, and there's water dripping out of it and leaving a track by the big stones.

CATHLEEN *in a whisper to the women who have come in:* Is it
    Bartley it is?
ONE OF THE WOMEN: It is, surely, God rest his soul.

*Two younger women come in and pull out the table. Then men
carry in the body of Bartley, laid on a plank, with a bit of a sail
over it, and lay it on the table.*

CATHLEEN *to the women as they are doing so:* What way was
    he drowned?
ONE OF THE WOMEN: The grey pony knocked him over into
    the sea, and he was washed out where there is a great surf
    on the white rocks.

*Maurya has gone over and knelt down at the head of the table.
The women are keening softly and swaying themselves with a
slow movement. Cathleen and Nora kneel at the other end of
the table. The men kneel near the door.*

MAURYA *raising her head and speaking as if she did not see the
    people around her:* They're all gone now, and there isn't
    anything more the sea can do to me. . . . I'll have no call
    now to be up crying and praying when the wind breaks
    from the south, and you can hear the surf is in the east,
    and the surf is in the west, making a great stir with the
    two noises, and they hitting one on the other. I'll have
    no call now to be going down and getting Holy Water in
    the dark nights after Samhain, and I won't care what way
    the sea is when the other women will be keening. *To
    Nora.* Give me the Holy Water, Nora; there's a small sup
    still on the dresser.

Nora gives it to her.

    *Drops Michael's clothes across Bartley's feet, and sprinkles
    the Holy Water over him.* It isn't that I haven't prayed
    for you, Bartley, to the Almighty God. It isn't that I
    haven't said prayers in the dark night till you wouldn't
    know what I'd be saying; but it's a great rest I'll have

now, and it's time, surely. It's a great rest I'll have now, and great sleeping in the long nights after Samhain, if it's only a bit of wet flour we do have to eat, and maybe a fish that would be stinking. *She kneels down again, crossing herself, and saying prayers under her breath.*

CATHLEEN *to an old man:* Maybe yourself and Eamon would make a coffin when the sun rises. We have fine white boards herself bought, God help her, thinking Michael would be found, and I have a new cake you can eat while you'll be working.

THE OLD MAN *looking at the boards:* Are there nails with them?

CATHLEEN: There are not, Colum; we didn't think of the nails.

ANOTHER MAN: It's a great wonder she wouldn't think of the nails, and all the coffins she's seen made already.

CATHLEEN: It's getting old she is, and broken.

Maurya stands up again very slowly and spreads out the pieces of Michael's clothes beside the body, sprinkling them with the last of the Holy Water.

NORA *in a whisper to Cathleen:* She's quiet now and easy; but the day Michael was drowned you could hear her crying out from this to the spring well. It's fonder she was of Michael, and would any one have thought that?

CATHLEEN *slowly and clearly:* An old woman will be soon tired with anything she will do, and isn't it nine days herself is after crying and keening, and making great sorrow in the house?

MAURYA *puts the empty cup mouth downwards on the table, and lays her hands together on Bartley's feet:* They're all together this time, and the end is come. May the Almighty God have mercy on Bartley's soul, and on Michael's soul, and on the souls of Sheamus and Patch, and Stephen and Shawn (*bending her head*); and may He have mercy on my soul, Nora, and on the soul of every one is left living in the world.

She pauses, and the keen rises a little more loudly from the women, then sinks away.

> *Continuing.* Michael has a clean burial in the far north, by the grace of the Almighty God. Bartley will have a fine coffin out of the white boards, and a deep grave surely. What more can we want than that? No man at all can be living for ever, and we must be satisfied.

She kneels down again and the curtain falls slowly.

The Wayfarer

Patrick Pearse

Written by Pearse on the day before his execution, this little poem is very moving and a strong counterblast to charges of a deliberately engineered martyrdom.

The beauty of the world hath made me sad,
This beauty that will pass;
Sometimes my heart hath shaken with great joy
To see a leaping squirrel in a tree,
Or a red lady-bird upon a stalk,
Or little rabbits in a field at evening,
Lit by a slanting sun,
Or some green hill where shadows drifted by,
Some quiet hill where mountainy man hath sown
And soon will reap, near to the gate of Heaven;
Or children with bare feet upon the sands
Of some ebbed sea, or playing on the streets
Of little towns in Connacht,
Things young and happy.
And then my heart hath told me:
These will pass,
Will pass and change, will die and be no more,
Things bright and green, things young and happy;
And I have gone upon my way
Sorrowful.

A Soft Day

Winifred M. Letts

An evocation, famous for its first line of weather all too prevalent in Ireland but still capable of charming even the sodden natives.

A soft day, thank God!
A wind from the south
With a honeyed mouth;
A scent of drenching leaves,
Briar and beech and lime,
White elder-flower and thyme
And the soaking grass smells sweet,
Crushed by my two bare feet,
While the rain drips,
Drips, drips, drips from the eaves.

A soft day, thank God!
The hills wear a shroud
Of silver cloud;
The web the spider weaves
Is a glittering net;
The woodland path is wet,
And the soaking earth smells sweet
Under my two bare feet,
And the rain drips,
Drips, drips, drips from the leaves.

Me an' Me Da

W. F. Marshall

A cautionary tale from the Sperrin Mountains and famous
north of a line from Donegal Bay to Carlingford Lough.

I'm livin' in Drumlister,
   An' I'm gettin very oul',
I have to wear an Indian bag
   To save me from the coul'.
The deil a man in this townlan'
   Wos claner raired nor me,
But I'm livin' in Drumlister
   In clabber to the knee.

Me da lived up in Carmin,
   An' kep' a sarvint boy;
His second wife wos very sharp,
   He birried her with joy:
Now she wos thin, her name was Flynn,
   She comes from Cullentra,
An' if me shirt's a clatty shirt
   The man to blame's me da.

Consarnin' weemin, sure it wos
   A constant word of his,
"Keep far away from them that's thin,
   Their temper's aisy riz."
Well, I knowed two I thought wud do,
   But still I had me fears,
So I kiffled back an' forrit
   Between the two, for years.

Wee Margit had no fortune
   But two rosy cheeks wud plaze;
The farm of lan' wos Bridget's,
   But she tuk the pock disayse:
An' Margit she wos very wee,
   An' Bridget she wos stout,
But her face wos like a gaol dure
   With the bowlts pulled out.

I'll tell no lie on Margit,
   She thought the worl' of me;
I'll tell the thruth, me heart wud lep
   The sight of her to see.
But I wos slow, ye surely know,
   The raison of it now,
If I left her home from Carmin
   Me da wud rise a row.

So I swithered back an' forrit
   Till Margit got a man;
A fella come from Mullaslin
   An' left me jist the wan.
I mind the day she went away,
   I hid wan strucken hour,
An' cursed the wasp from Cullentra
   That made me da so sour.

But cryin' cures no trouble,
   To Bridget I went back,
An' faced her for it that night week
   Beside her own thurf-stack.
I axed her there, an' spoke her fair,
   The handy wife she'd make me,
I talked about the lan' that joined
   —Begob, she wudn't take me!

So I'm livin' in Drumlister,
   An' I'm gettin' very oul'
I creep to Carmin wanst a month
   To thry an' make me sowl:
The deil a man in this townlan'
   Wos claner raired nor me,
An' I'm dyin' in Drumlister
   In clabber to the knee.

Three Lovely Lasses in Bannion

Delia Murphy

One of Delia Murphy's most popular songs and assigned to
her as author. It has frequently been parodied, most notably
by Donagh MacDonagh in *Happy As Larry* as "Three Old
Ladies from Hades".

There are three lovely lasses in Bannion,
Bannion, Bannion, Bannion,
There are three lovely lassies in Bannion,
And I am the best of them all,
And I am the best of them all.

For my father has forty white shillings,
Shillings, shillings, shillings,
For my father has forty white shillings,
And the grass of a goat and a cow,
And the grass of a goat and a cow.

And my mother she says I can marry,
Marry, marry, marry,
My mother she says I can marry
And she'll leave me her bed when she dies,
And she'll leave me her bed when she dies.

So I'll send my old shoes to be mended,
Mended, mended, mended,
I'll send my old shoes to be mended
And my petticoat to be dyed green,
And my petticoat to be dyed green.

And on next Sunday morning I'll meet him,
Meet him, meet him, meet him,
On next Sunday morning I'll meet him
And I shall be dressed like a queen,
And I shall be dressed like a queen.

There are three lovely asses in Bannion,
Bannion, Bannion, Bannion,
There are three lovely asses in Bannion
To draw me on my wedding day,
To draw me on my wedding day.

Shancoduff

Patrick Kavanagh

Shancoduff and black hills eternally looking north towards
Armagh give the most personal view of the poet there is. The
line, "A poet? Then by heavens he must be poor" finds an
almost proverbial strength in literary circles.

My black hills have never seen the sun rising
Eternally they look north towards Armagh,
Lot's wife would not be salt if she had been
Incurious as my black hills that are happy
When dawn whitens Glassdrummond chapel.

My hills hoard the bright shillings of March
While the sun searches in every pocket.
They are my Alps and I have climbed the Matterhorn
With a sheaf of hay for three perishing calves
In the field under the Big Forth of Rocksavage.

The sleety winds fondle the rushy beards of Shancoduff
While the cattle-drovers sheltering in the Featherna Bush
Look up and say: 'Who owns them hungry hills
That the water-hen and snipe must have forsaken?
A poet? Then by heavens he must be poor.'
I hear and is my heart not badly shaken?

V

The Wild Freshness of Morning
Evening's Best Light

I Saw from the Beach

Thomas Moore

Though not Moore's best known melody it can be the most
effective of all his pieces as a concert item. The slight senti-
mentality and over-exposure of some of the other favourites
is missing here and it remains a genuinely touching statement
about youth and age.

I saw from the beach, when the morning was shining,
A bark o'er the waters move gloriously on;
I came when the sun o'er that beach was declining,
The bark was still there but the waters were gone.

And such is the fate of our life's early promise,
So passing the spring-tide of joy we have known;
Each wave, that we danc'd on at morning, ebbs from us,
And leaves us, at eve, on the bleak shore alone.

Ne'er tell me of glories, serenely adorning
The close of our day, the calm eve of our night—
Give me back, give me back, the wild freshness of morning,
Her clouds and her tears are worth evening's best light.

Oh, who would not welcome that moment's returning,
When passion first wak'd a new life through his frame,
And his soul, like the wood, that grows precious in
  burning,
Gave out all its sweets to love's exquisite flame.

The Last Rose of Summer

Thomas Moore

So well known was this symbolic tale and so effective the melody that Flotow incorporated it in his opera, *Martha*, in 1847.

'Tis the last rose of summer, left blooming alone;
All her lovely companions are faded and gone,
No flow'r of her kindred, no rose bud is nigh,
To reflect back her blushes, or give sigh for sigh.

I'll not leave thee, thou lone one! to pine on the stem:
Since the lovely are sleeping, go, sleep thou with them,
Thus kindly I scatter thy leaves o'er the bed.
Where thy mates of the garden lie scentless and dead.

So soon may I follow, when friendships decay,
And from love's shining circle the gems drop away.
When true hearts lie wither'd and fond ones are flown,
Oh! who would inhabit this bleak world alone!

The Dying Girl

Richard d'Alton Williams

A poem whose immortality is based upon the last two lines of the first verse. It was one of the great sob-pieces of nineteenth-century entertainment.

From a Munster vale they brought her,
   From the pure and balmy air;
An Ormond peasant's daughter,
   With blue eyes and golden hair.
They brought her to the city
   And she faded slowly there—
Consumption has no pity
   For blue eyes and golden hair.

When I saw her first reclining
   Her lips were mov'd in prayer,
And the setting sun was shining
   On her loosen'd golden hair.
When our kindly glances met her,
   Deadly brilliant was her eye;
And she said that she was better,
   While we knew that she must die.

She speaks of Munster valleys,
   The pattern, dance, and fair,
And her thin hand feebly dallies
   With her scattered golden hair.
When silently we listen'd
   To her breath with quiet care,
Her eyes with wonder glisten'd,
   And she asked us, "What was there?"

The poor thing smiled to ask it,
   And her pretty mouth laid bare,
Like gems within a casket,
   A string of pearlets rare.
We said that we were trying
   By the gushing of her blood
And the time she took in sighing
   To know if she were good.

Well, she smil'd and chatted gaily,
   Though we saw in mute despair
The hectic brighter daily,
   And the death-dew on her hair.
And oft her wasted fingers
   Beating time upon the bed:
O'er some old tune she lingers,
   And she bows her golden head.

At length the harp is broken;
   And the spirit in its strings,
As the last decree is spoken,
   To its source exulting springs.
Descending swiftly from the skies
   Her guardian angel came,
He struck God's lightning from her eyes,
   And bore Him back the flame.

Before the sun had risen
   Through the lark-loved morning air,
Her young soul left its prison,
   Undefiled by sin or care.
I stood beside the couch in tears
   Where pale and calm she slept,
And though I've gazed on death for years,
   I blush not that I wept.

I check'd with effort pity's sighs
  And left the matron there,
To close the curtains of her eyes
  And bind her golden hair.

The Fairies *(A Child's Song)*

William Allingham

Allingham's most famous poem was written when he was twenty-five, at Killybegs, the fishing port on the south coast of Donegal. He was a customs officer and the poem was written on a tour of duty. The site is very close to the path of the old king on his journey. "Columbkill" is Glencolmcille in south-west Donegal. The fairies are the benevolent creatures of Victorian picture-books, leagues away from the malevolent and rather dangerous *Daoine Beaga* of Irish folklore.

Up the airy mountain,
    Down the rushy glen,
We daren't go a-hunting
    For fear of little men;
Wee folk, good folk,
    Trooping all together;
Green jacket, red cap,
    And white owl's feather!

Down along the rocky shore
    Some make their home—
They live on crispy pancakes
    Of yellow tide-foam;
Some in the reeds
    Of the black mountain lake,
With frogs for their watch-dogs,
    All night awake.

High on the hill-top
    The old King sits;
He is now so old and grey
    He's nigh lost his wits.

With a bridge of white mist
  Columbkill he crosses,
On his stately journeys
  From Slieveleague to Rosses;
Or going up with music
  On cold starry nights,
To sup with the Queen
  Of the gay Northern Lights.

They stole little Bridget
  For seven years long;
When she came down again
  Her friends were all gone.
They took her lightly back,
  Between the night and morrow;
They thought that she was fast asleep,
  But she was dead with sorrow
They have kept her ever since
  Deep within the lake,
On a bed of flag-leaves,
  Watching till she wake.

By the craggy hill-side,
  Through the mosses bare,
They have planted thorn-trees
  For pleasure here and there.
Is any man so daring
  As dig one up in spite,
He shall find their sharpest thorns
  In his bed at night.

Up the airy mountain,
  Down the rushy glen,
We daren't go a-hunting
  For fear of little men;
Wee folk, good folk,
  Trooping all together;
Green jacket, red cap,
  And white owl's feather!

Bantry Bay

James Lynam Molloy

J. L. Molloy's other great song sharing its fame with "The Kerry Dance". The song is popular with amateur tenors but the change of tune in the third verse foxes all but the very best.

As I'm sitting all alone in the gloaming,
It might have been but yesterday,
That we watched the fisher sails all homing,
Till the little herring fleet at anchor lay.
Then the fisher girls with baskets swinging,
Came running down the old stone way,
Every lassie to her sailor lad was singing,
A welcome back to Bantry Bay.

Then we heard the piper's sweet note tuning,
And all the lassies turned to hear:
As they mingled with a soft voice crooning,
Till the music floated down the wooden pier,
"Save you kindly colleens all," said the piper,
"Hands across and trip it while I play,"
And a tender sound of song and merry dancing,
Stole softly over Bantry Bay.

As I'm sitting all alone in the gloaming,
The shadows of the past draw near.
And I see the loving faces round me
That used to glad the old brown pier.
Some are gone up on their last lov'd homing,
Some are left, but they are old and grey,
And we're waiting for the tide in the gloaming,
To sail up on the Great High-way,
To the land of rest unending,
All peacefully from Bantry Bay.

If I Was a Lady

Percy French

A typical monologue of the kind that formed the programme of a Percy French travelling entertainment. He and a lady partner (for a lot of his career, May Laffan) would provide a mixed grill of songs, monologues, banjo-duets and painting of water-colours and smoke pictures on plates.

If I was a lady, I'd wear a hat
That all the street would be lookin' at,
An' I'd have a ladies' maid, d'ye mind,
To lace and button me dress behind.
A dress that was lined with good sateen,
None o' yer bits o' bombazine,
And the girls with envy would grind their teeth,
When they heard it rustling underneath.
If I was a lady—but then I'm not,
This shawl is the dacentest thing I've got.

If I was a lady I'd drive to the play,
An' I'd look through me opera glass and say—
"I've seen this silly revue before,
The leading lady's an awful bore;
Let's all get up when she starts her song,
An' go an' eat cakes in a resterong."
Then a powder puff on me nose I'd dab,
An' drive off home in a taxi cab,
If I was a lady—but then I'm not,
A pass to the gallery's all I've got.

If I was a lady—a regular swell,
With a hairy boa, an' a silk umbrel',
'Tis me that would walk into Shelbourne's Hotel,

An' order me dinner—"Some pork an' beans,
An' whatever ye've got in them soup turreens,
Both the sweets, an' a hunk o' cheese,
And oh, a bottle o' porter please."
Then I'd call for me bill and setteling it,
I'd give the waiter a threepenny bit,
If I was a lady—but then I'm not,
—My dinner comes out o' the stirabout pot.
Still there's a lot of show and sham,
Maybe I'm safer the way I am.

The Gartan Mother's Lullaby

Joseph Campbell

One of the best of modern Irish lullabies based upon the *suantrai* model from the Gaelic. Gartan is a lake in central Donegal.

Sleep, O babe, for the red bee hums
The silent twilight's fall.
Aoibheall from the Grey Rock comes
To wrap the world in thrall.
A leanbhan o, my child, my joy,
My love and heart's desire;
The crickets sing you lullaby,
Beside the dying fire.

Dusk is drawn, and the Green Man's thorn
Is wreathed in rings of joy;
Siobhra sails his boat till morn
Upon the starry bog.
A leanbhan o, the paly moon,
Hath brimm'd her cusp in dew
And weeps to hear the sad sleep tune I sing,
O love to you.

Sleep, O babe, for the red bee hums,
The silent twilight's fall.
Aoibheall from the Grey Rock comes
To wrap the world in thrall.
A leanbhan van o, my child, my joy,
My love and heart's desire,
The crickets sing you lullaby,
Beside the dying fire.

I Shall Not Go to Heaven

Helen Waddell

One of the few poems written by the Belfast-born medievalist
and novelist. It is set, so to speak, in the Mourne Mountains.

I shall not go to Heaven when I die,
    But if they let me be
I think I'll take the road I used to know
    That goes by Shere-na-garagh and the sea.
And all day breasting me the wind shall blow,
    And I'll hear nothing but the peewits cry
And the waves talking in the sea below.

I think it will be winter when I die
    For no one from the North could die in spring—
And all the heather will be dead and grey
    And the bog-cotton will have blown away,
And there will be no yellow on the whin.

But I shall smell the peat,
    And when it's almost dark I'll set my feet
Where a white track goes glimmering to the hills,
    And see far up a light. . . .
Would you think Heaven could be so small a thing
    As a lit window on the hills at night?
And come in stumbling from the gloom,
    Half-blind, into a fire-lit room,
Turn, and see you,
    And there abide.

If it were true
    And if I thought they would let me be
I almost wish it were tonight I died.

My Aunt Jane

Anonymous

The Belfast child's national anthem but known throughout
the North. A version of the tune was used as signature music
for Joseph Tomelty's long-running radio series of the fifties,
The McCooeys.

My aunt Jane, she took me in.
She gave me tea out o' her wee tin
Half a bap and a wee snow top
And cinnamon buds out o' her wee shop.

My aunt Jane has a bell at the door
A white step-stone and a clean-swept floor
Candy-apples and hard green pears
And conversation lozengers.

My aunt Jane can dance a jig
And sing a ballad round a sweetie pig
Wee red eyes, and a cord for a tail
Hanging in a bunch from a farthing nail.

My aunt Jane she's awful smart
She bakes a ring in an apple tart
And when that Hallow E'en comes round
Fornenst that tart I'm always found.

A Christmas Childhood

Patrick Kavanagh

Kavanagh, for all his awkwardness and abruptness, was a very
soft and sensitive creature underneath. The wonder and child's
vision of the world, as seen in this poem, never left him.

I

One side of the potato-pits was white with frost—
How wonderful that was, how wonderful!
And when we put our ears to the paling-post
The music that came out was magical.

The light between the ricks of hay and straw
Was a hole in Heaven's gable. An apple tree
With its December-glinting fruit we saw—
O you, Eve, were the world that tempted me

To eat the knowledge that grew in clay
And death the germ within it! Now and then
I can remember something of the gay
Garden that was childhood's. Again

The tracks of cattle to a drinking-place,
A green stone lying sideways in a ditch
Or any common sight the transfigured face
Of a beauty that the world did not touch.

II

My father played the melodeon
Outside at our gate;
There were stars in the morning east
And they danced to his music.

Across the wild bogs his melodeon called
to Lennons and Callans.
As I pulled on my trousers in a hurry
I knew some strange thing had happened.

Outside the cow-house my mother
Made the music of milking;
The light of her stable-lamp was a star
And the frost of Bethlehem made it twinkle.

A water-hen screeched in the bog,
Mass-going feet
Crunched the wafer-ice on the pot-holes,
Somebody wistfully twisted the bellows wheel.

My child poet picked out the letters
On the grey stone,
In silver the wonder of a Christmas townland,
The winking glitter of a frosty dawn.

Cassiopeia was over
Cassidy's hanging hill,
I looked and three whin bushes rode across
The horizon—the Three Wise Kings.

An old man passing said:
'Can't he make it talk'—
The melodeon. I hid in the doorway
And tightened the belt of my box-pleated coat.

I nicked six nicks on the door-post
With my penknife's big blade—
There was a little one for cutting tobacco.
And I was six Christmases of age.

My father played the melodeon,
My mother milked the cows,
And I had a prayer like a white rose pinned
On the Virgin Mary's blouse.

Wee Hughie

Elizabeth Shane

A poem from Donegal, written by a vicar's daughter, well known by most adults over forty.

He's gone to school, Wee Hughie,
An' him not four,
Sure I saw the fright was in him
When he left the door.

But he took a hand of Denny
An' a hand of Dan,
Wi' Joe's owld coat upon him—
Och, the poor wee man!

He cut the quarest figure,
More stout nor thin,
An' trottin' right an' steady,
Wi' his toes turned in

I watched him to the corner
O' the big turf stack,
An' the more his feet went forrit,
Still his head turned back.

He was lookin', would I call him,
Och, me heart was woe—
Sure it's lost I am without him,
But he be to go.

I followed to the turnin'
When he passed it by,
God help him, he was cryin'
And maybe so was I.

VI

I Know My Love

Cailín Deas Crúite na mBó
(The Pretty Milkmaid)

Anonymous

The Irish title and refrain was used by Dion Boucicault who always had an ear for a good tune and an actor-manager's instinct as to when and where to introduce it in a play. It helps ease the tension of his most famous melodrama, *The Colleen Bawn*. George M. Cohan, the Yankee Doodle-Dandy, used a jazzed-up version in his Broadway show, *Little Nelly Kelly*.

It was on a fine summer's morning,
When the birds sweetly tuned on each bow,
I heard a fair maid sing most charming.
As she sat a-milking her cow;
Her voice it was chanting melodious,
She left me scarce able to go,
My heart it is soothed in solace,
My Cailín deas crúite na mBó.

With courtesy I did salute her,
"Good-morrow most amiable maid,
I'm your captive slave for the future."
"Kind sir, do not banter," she said,
"I'm not such a precious rare jewel,
That I should enamour you so,
I am but a plain country girl,"
Says Cailín deas crúite na mBó.

"The Indies afford no such jewels,
So precious and transparently fair,
Oh! do not to my flame add fuel,
But consent for to love me my dear,
Take pity and grant my desire,

And leave me no longer in woe,
Oh! love me or else I'll expire,
Sweet Cailín deas crúite na mBó.

"Or had I the wealth of great Damer,
Or all on the African shore,
Or had I great Devonshire treasure,
Or had I ten thousand times more,
Or had I the lamp of Alladin,
Or had I his genie also,
I'd rather live poor on a mountain,
With Cailín deas crúite na mBó."

"I beg you'll withdraw and don't tease me
I cannot consent unto thee,
I like to live single and airy,
Till more of the world I do see,
New cares they would me embarrass
Besides, sir, my fortune is low,
Until I get rich I'll not marry,"
Says Cailín deas crúite na mBó.

"An old maid is like an old almanack,
Quite useless when once out of date,
If her ware is not sold in the morning
At noon it must fall to low rate,
The fragrance of May is soon over,
The rose loses its beauty you know,
All bloom is consumed in October,
Sweet Cailín deas crúite na mBó.

"A young maid is like a ship sailing,
There's no knowing how long she may steer,
For with every blast she's in danger,
Oh consent love and banish all care,
For riches I care not a farthing,
Your affection I want and no more
In comfort I'd wish to enjoy you,
My Cailín deas crúite na mBó."

The Enniskillen Dragoon

Anonymous

Susceptibility to the attraction of a redcoat seems to have been
as prevalent in Ireland as anywhere else. One of many soldiers
songs from the tradition.

A beautiful damsel of fame and renown,
A gentleman's daughter near Monaghan town,
As she rode by the barracks, this beautiful maid,
She stood in her coach to see dragoons on parade.

They were all dressed like gentlemen's sons,
With their bright shining swords and their carabine guns,
With their silver-mounted pistols she observed them full
        soon,
Because she loved her Enniskillen dragoon.

You bright sons of Mars that stand on the right,
Outshines the armour of bright stars by night,
Saying Willy, dearest Willy, you have listed full soon,
To serve in the Royal Enniskillen dragoon.

O beautiful Flora, your pardon I crave,
Now and for ever I will be your slave,
Your parents have slighted you morning and noon,
For fear that you'd wed your Enniskillen dragoon.

O Willy, dearest Willy, never mind what they say,
For children are bound their parents to obey,
When we're leaving Ireland they'll change their tune,
Saying the Lord may be with the Enniskillen dragoon.

Farewell, Enniskillen, farewell for a while,
And all round the borders of Erin's green isle,
When the war is over we'll return in full bloom,
And they'll all welcome home the Enniskillen dragoon.

Kitty of Coleraine

Charles Dawson Shanly
Edward Lysaght

A famous song with two mute claimants for authorship. It is
not in the folk tradition but a kind of aristocratic idyll like
"The Lass With The Delicate Air" and "Cherry Ripe" which
seems to suggest an eighteenth-century origin and the likelier
authorship of Lysaght.

As beautiful Kitty one morning was tripping
    With a pitcher of milk for the fair of Coleraine,
When she saw me she stumbled, the pitcher down tumbled,
    And all the sweet buttermilk watered the plain.
"Oh, what shall I do now? 'Twas looking at you now!
    I'm sure such a pitcher I'll ne'er see again.
'Twas the pride of my dairy. Oh, Barney McCleary,
    You're sent as a plague to the girls of Coleraine."

I sat down beside her, and gently did chide her
    That such a misfortune should give her such pain;
A kiss then I gave her, and before I did leave her
    She vowed for such pleasure she'd break it again.
'Twas the haymaking season—I can't tell the reason—
    Misfortunes will never come single, 'tis plain!
For very soon after poor Kitty's disaster
    The devil a pitcher was whole in Coleraine.

I Know My Love

Anonymous

"An old and antique song", but very elegant and from Cork.

I know my love by his way of walking,
And I know my love by his way of talking,
And I know my love dressed in his jersey blue,
And if my love leaves me, what will I do?

Chorus
And still she cried, "I love him best,
And a tiring mind can know no rest,"
And still she cried, "Bonny boys are few.
And if my love leaves me what will I do?"

There is a dance house down in Mardyke,
And there my true love goes every night,
And takes a strange one upon his knee,
And don't you think now that vexes me?

Chorus

Kathleen Mavourneen

Julia Crawford

Early nineteenth-century favourite written by Julia Crawford
and so famous over the years because of its seventh and ninth
lines that its title has become a euphemism for Hire Purchase
debt.

Kathleen Mavourneen! the grey dawn is breaking,
The horn of the hunter is heard on the hill;
The lark from her light wing the bright dew is shaking,
Kathleen Mavourneen! what, slumb'ring still?
Oh! hast thou forgotten how soon we must sever?
Oh! hast thou forgotten this day we must part?
It may be for years, and it may be forever,
Oh, why art thou silent, thou voice of my heart?
It may be for years, and it may be forever,
Then why art thou silent, Kathleen Mavourneen?

Kathleen Mavourneen! awake from thy slumbers,
The blue mountains glow in the sun's golden light,
Ah! where is the spell that once hung on thy numbers,
Arise in thy beauty, thou star of my light.
Mavourneen, Mavourneen, my sad tears are falling,
To think that from Erin and thee I must part;
It may be for years, and it may be forever;
Then why art thou silent, thou voice of my heart?
It may be for years, and it may be for ever;
Then why art thou silent, Kathleen Mavourneen?

The Rose of Aranmore

Anonymous

Aranmore is a largish island off the Rosses of Donegal. The song has been popular as a waltz and sing-song item for fifty years.

My thoughts to-day, though I'm far away,
Dwell on Tyrconnell's shore,
The salt sea air and the colleens fair
Of lovely green Gweedore.
There's a flower there, beyond compare,
That I'll treasure ever more,
That grand colleen, in her gown of green,
She's the Rose of Aranmore.

I've travelled far 'neath the Northern star,
Since the day I said good-bye;
And seen many maids in the golden glades
Beneath a tropic sky.
There's a vision in my reverie,
I always will adore,
That grand colleen, in her gown of green,
She's the Rose of Aranmore.

But soon I will return again
To the scenes I loved so well,
Where many an Irish lad and lass
Their tales of love do tell;
The silvery dunes and blue lagoons,
Along the Rosses shore
And that grand colleen, in her gown of green,
She's the Rose of Aranmore.

My Mary of the Curling Hair

Gerald Griffin

A love song by the author of *The Collegians* very popular
with tenors. The Irish elements ("*Siúl, Siúl, Siúl, a Ghrá.
Siúl go socair agus siúl go ciúin*"—Walk, my love; walk
calmly and safely) are to be found in several songs of the
period.

My Mary of the curling hair,
   The laughing teeth and bashful air,
Our bridal morn is dawning fair,
   With blushes in the skies!

Chorus
Shule, Shule, Shule Agra,
Shule a socar agus shule aroon!
My love, my pearl, my own dear girl
My mountain maid, arise!

For we were known from infancy,
   Thy father's hearth was home to me,
No selfish love was mine for thee,
   Unholy and unwise.

Chorus

I am no stranger proud and gay
   To win thee from thy home away,
And find thee for a distant day
   A theme for wasting sighs.

Chorus

But soon my love shall be my bride,
  And happy by our own fireside
My veins shall feel the rosy tide
  Which lingering hope denies.

Chorus

The Spinning Wheel

John Francis Waller

One of a handful of Irish songs that have international fame
and are not despised by the finest singers.

Mellow the moonlight to shine is beginning,
Close by the window young Eileen is spinning;
Bent o'er the fire her blind grandmother, sitting,
Is crooning and moaning and drowsily knitting.

Chorus
Merrily, cheerily, noiselessly, whirring,
Swings the wheel, spins the wheel, while the foot's stirring,
Sprightly and brightly and airily ringing
Thrills the sweet voice of the young maiden singing.

"Eileen, a chara, I hear someone tapping,"
" 'Tis the ivy, dear mother, against the glass flapping,"
"Eily, I surely hear somebody sighing,"
" 'Tis the sound, mother dear, of the summer winds dying."

Chorus

"What's that noise that I hear at the window, I wonder?"
" 'Tis the little birds chirping the holly-bush under,"
"What makes you be shoving and moving your stool on?
"And singing all wrong that old song of 'The Coolin'?"

Chorus

There's a form at the casement, the form of her true love,
And he whispers with face bent "I'm waiting for you, love"
"Get up on the stool, through the lattice step lightly,
We'll rove in the grove while the moon's shining brightly."

Chorus

The maid shakes her head, on her lips lays her fingers,
Steals up from her seat, longs to go and yet lingers;
A frightened glance turns to her drowsy grandmother,
Puts one foot on the stool, spins the wheel with the other.

Chorus

Lazily, easily, swings now the wheel round,
Slowly and lowly is heard now the reel's sound;
Noiseless and light to the lattice above her
The maid steps, then leaps to the arms of her lover.

Chorus

Slower, and slower, and slower the wheel swings,
Lower, and lower, and lower the reel rings;
Ere the reel and the wheel stopped their ringing and moving,
Through the grove the young lovers by moonlight are roving.

The Lark in the Clear Air

Samuel Ferguson

Original words written to an old Irish tune called "The Tailor"
during Ferguson's brief nationalist phase have made this one
of the most beautiful of all Irish songs.

Dear thoughts are in my mind, and my soul soars enchanted,
As I hear the sweet lark sing, in the clear air of the day,
For a tender beaming smile to my hope has been granted,
And to-morrow she shall hear all my fond heart would say.

I shall tell her all my love, all my soul's adoration.
And I think she will hear me, and will not say me nay;
It is this that gives my soul all its joyous elation,
As I hear the sweet lark sing, in the clear air of the day.

Carrigdhoun
(Lament of the Irish Maiden)

Denny Lane

The most popular song of Denny Lane, the Cork engineer who finished his career as President of the Institute of Gas Engineers of Great Britain. The tune was adapted as the music for Percy French's "The Mountains of Mourne" by Dr Collisson.

The heath was green in Carrigdhoun,
   Bright shone the sun on Ardnalee,
The dark green trees bent trembling down,
   To kiss the slumbering Owenabwee,
That happy day, 'twas but last May,
   'Tis like a dream to me,
When Domhnal swore aye, o'er and o'er,
   We'll part no more astór mo chroidhe

On Carrigdhoun the heath is brown,
   The clouds are dark over Ardnalee,
And many a stream comes rushing down
   To swell the angry Owenabwee.
The moaning blast is sweeping fast
   Thru' many a leafless tree,
And I'm alone, for he is gone,
   My hawk is flown, ochone machree!

Soft April showers and bright May flowers
   Will bring the summer back again;
But will they bring me back the hours
   I spent with my brave Domhnal then?
'Tis but a chance, for he's gone to France
   To wear the fleur-de-lis;
But I'll follow you, my Domhnal dhu,
   For still I'm true to you, a chroidhe

The Rose of Tralee

William Pembroke Mulchinock

The song most likely to be sung by an Irish drunk if the mood is romantic (if patriotic it will be "Kevin Barry"). Mulchinock was a Protestant and a contributor to the *Nation*. "Mary" was Mary O'Connor, the servant girl with whom he fell in love and who afterwards died of tuberculosis.

The pale moon was rising above the green mountain,
　The sun was declining beneath the blue sea,
When I stray'd with my love to the pure crystal fountain
　That stands in the beautiful vale of Tralee.

She was lovely and fair as the rose of the summer,
　Yet 'twas not her beauty alone that won me,
Oh, no, 'twas the truth in her eyes ever beaming
　That made me love Mary, the Rose of Tralee.

The cool shades of evening their mantle were spreading,
　And Mary, all smiling, was list'ning to me,
The moon through the valley her pale rays was shedding
　When I won the heart of the Rose of Tralee.

Tho' lovely and fair as the rose of the summer,
　Yet 'twas not her beauty alone that won me,
Oh, no, 'twas the truth in her eyes ever beaming
　That made me love Mary, the Rose of Tralee.

Slievenamon

Charles J. Kickham

Kickham came from Mullinahone, County Tipperary, a region which, like Japan with Fujiyama and the Rosses with Errigal, regards Sliabh na mBan (The Women's Mountain) as a kind of magic mountain. The element of nationalism in verse three is entirely appropriate from the pen of a life-long Fenian.

Alone, all alone, by the wave-wash'd strand,
And alone in the crowded hall.
The hall it is gay, and the waves they are grand,
But my heart is not here at all!
It flies far away, by night and by day,
To the time and the joys that are gone!
And I never can forget the sweet maiden I met,
In the Valley near Slievenamon.

It was not the grace of her queenly air,
Nor her cheek of the rose's glow,
Nor her soft black eyes, nor her flowing hair,
Nor was it her lily-white brow.
'Twas the soul of truth and of melting ruth,
And the smile like a Summer dawn,
That stole my heart away one soft Summer day,
In the Valley near Slievenamon.

In the festive hall, by the star-watch'd shore,
Ever my restless spirit cries:
"My love, oh, my love, shall I ne'er see you more?
And, my land, will you never uprise?"
By night and by day, I ever, ever, pray,
While lonely my life flows on,
To see our flag unrolled, and my true love to enfold,
In the Valley near Slievenamon.

I'll Sing Thee Songs of Araby

W. G. Wills

A perfect example of the soirée song, a parlour gem for
after-dinner performance adaptable for both sexes. Wills was
born in Kilkenny.

I'll sing thee songs of Araby,
   And tales of fair Cashmere,
Wild tales to cheat thee of a sigh,
   Or charm thee to a tear.
And dreams of delight shall on thee break,
   And rainbow visions rise,
And all my soul shall strive to wake
   Sweet wonder in thine eyes!

Through those twin lakes, when wonder wakes,
   My raptur'd song shall sink,
And as the diver dives for pearls,
   Bring tears, bright tears to their brink;
And dreams of delight shall on thee break,
   And rainbow visions rise,
And all my soul shall strive to wake
   Sweet wonder in thine eyes,
To cheat thee of a sigh
   Or charm thee to a tear!

The Garden Where the Praties Grow

Johnny Patterson

Another intensely popular song from the hands of Ireland's favourite nineteenth-century clown who also wrote "The Stone Outside Dan Murphy's Door" and "The Old Turf Fire".

Have you ever been in love, me boys,
Oh! have you felt the pain,
I'd rather be in jail, I would,
Than be in love again;
Tho' the girl I loved was beautiful,
I'd have you all to know,
That I met her in the garden
Where the praties grow.

Chorus
She was just the sort of creature now,
That nature did intend
To walk right thro' the world me boys
Without the Grecian bend.
Nor did she wear a chignon
I'd have you all to know.
And I met her in the garden
Where the praties grow.

She was singing an old Irish song
Called "Gradh Geal mo Chroidhe,"
"Oh boys", says I, "what a wife she'd make
For an Irish lad like me."
I was on important business but
I did not like to go,
And leave the girl and garden
Where the praties grow.

216

Chorus

Says I, "My lovely colleen,
I hope you'll pardon me,"
But she wasn't like those city girls
Who'd say, "You're making free."
She answered then right modestly,
And curtsied very low,
Saying, "You're welcome to the garden
Where the praties grow."

Chorus

Says I, "My lovely darling
I'm tired of single life,
And if you've no objections,
I'll make you my sweet wife."
Says she, "I'll ask my parents,
And to-morrow I'll let you know,
If you'll meet me in the garden
Where the praties grow."

Chorus

Now her parents they consented,
And we're blessed with children three,
Two girls just like their mother,
And a boy the image of me;
We'll train them up in decency
The way they ought to go;
But I'll ne'er forget the garden
Where the praties grow.

Chorus

Maire, My Girl

John Keegan Casey

Casey's famous love song was written in honour of Mary
Donnelly, a girl from Ballynacargy, Co. Westmeath, whom
he knew when she was teaching in Forgney National School.
The last line of every verse is repeated in singing.

Over the dim blue hills strays a wild river,
Over the dim blue hills rests my heart ever,
Dearer and brighter than jewels and pearls,
Dwells she in beauty there, Maire, my girl.

Down upon Claris heath shines the soft berry,
On the brown harvest tree droops the red cherry.
Sweeter thy honey lips, softer the curl,
Straying adown thy cheeks, Maire, my girl.

'Twas on an April eve that I first met her;
Many an eve shall pass ere I forget her.
Since my young heart has been wrapped in a whirl,
Thinking and dreaming of Maire my girl.

She is too kind and fond ever to grieve me,
She has too pure a heart e'er to deceive me.
Were I Tyrconnell's chief or Desmond's earl,
Life would be dark, wanting Maire my girl.

Over the dim blue hills strays a wild river,
Over the dim blue hills rests my heart ever.
Fairer and dearer than jewel or pearl,
Dwells she in beauty there, Maire my girl.

Trottin' to the Fair

A. P. Graves

One of A. P. Graves's better songs, called by him "Riding Double" but now much better known by its first line.

Trottin' to the fair
Me and Moll Maloney,
Seated I declare,
On a single pony.

How am I to know that
Molly's safe behind,
With our heads in
Oh, that awkward, awkward way inclined.

By her gentle breathing
Whispered past my ear
And her white arms wreathin'
Warm around me here.

Thus on Dobbin's back
I discoursed the darling
Till up on the track
Leaped a mongrel snarling.

'Ah,' says Moll, 'I'm frightened, frightened,
That the pony'll start.'
And her pretty hands she tightened
Round my happy heart.

Till I axed her, 'May I
Steal a kiss or so?'
And my Molly's grey eye
Didn't answer no.

Gortnamona

Percy French

A poem written by French in memory of his first wife, Ettie,
who died in childbirth. Brendan O'Dowda, French's modern
interpreter, persuaded Philip Green to set it to music and it
has become a very popular and unusual "French" song.

Long, long ago in the woods of Gortnamona,
 I thought the birds were singing in the blackthorn tree;
 But oh! it was my heart that was ringing, ringing,
   ringing,
 With the joy that you were bringing O my love, to me.

Long, long ago, in the woods of Gortnamona,
 I thought the wind was sighing round the blackthorn
    tree;
But oh! it was the banshee that was crying, crying, crying,
 And I knew my love was dying far across the sea.

Now if you go through the woods of Gortnamona,
 You hear the raindrops creeping through the blackthorn
   tree.
But oh! it is the tears I am weeping, weeping, weeping,
 For the loved one that is sleeping far away from me.

John-John

Thomas MacDonagh

One of MacDonagh's most beautiful love poems, often justly
anthologised.

I dreamt last night of you, John-John,
   And thought you called to me;
And when I woke this morning, John,
   Yourself I hoped to see;
But I was all alone, John-John,
   Though still I heard your call:
I put my boots and bonnet on,
   And took my Sunday shawl,
And went, full sure to find you, John,
         To Nenagh fair.

The fair was just the same as then,
   Five years ago to-day,
When first you left the thimble men
   And came with me away;
For there again were thimble men
   And shooting galleries,
And card-trick men and Maggie men
   Of all sorts and degrees—
But not a sight of you, John-John,
         Was anywhere.

I turned my face to home again,
   And called myself a fool
To think you'd leave the thimble men
   And live again by rule,
And go to mass and keep the fast
   And till the little patch:
My wish to have you home was past

Before I raised the latch
And pushed the door and saw you, John,
   Sitting down there.

How cool you came in here, begad,
 As if you owned the place!
But rest yourself there now, my lad,
 'Tis good to see your face;
My dream is out, and now by it
 I think I know my mind:
At six o'clock this house you'll quit,
 And leave no grief behind;—
But until six o'clock, John-John,
   My bit you'll share.

My neighbours' shame of me began
 When first I brought you in;
To wed and keep a tinker man
 They thought a kind of sin;
But now this three year since you're gone
 'Tis pity me they do,
And that I'd rather have John-John,
 Than that they'd pity you.
Pity for me and you, John-John,
   I could not bear.

Oh, you're my husband right enough,
 But what's the good of that?
You know you never were the stuff
 To be the cottage cat,
To watch the fire and hear me lock
 The door and put out Shep—
But there now, it is six o'clock
 And time for you to step.
God bless and keep you far, John-John!
   And that's my prayer.

Golden Stockings

Oliver St John Gogarty

Buck Mulligan in a lyrical mood and showing that he was a much better poet than Stephen Dedalus.

Golden stockings you had on
In the meadow where you ran;
And your little knees together
Bobbed like pippins in the weather
When the breezes rush and fight
For those dimples of delight;
And they dance from the pursuit,
And the leaf looks like the fruit.

I have many a sight in mind
That would last if I were blind;
Many verses I could write
That would bring me many a sight.
Now I only see but one,
See you running in the sun;
And the gold-dust coming up
From the trampled butter-cup.

My Lagan Love

Joseph Campbell

A great feis bass test-piece, sung with a plethora of grace-notes. It has not been established which Lagan is in question, the basin of Belfast's decorous river or the fertile Lagan valley of east Donegal and west Tyrone. Campbell was a Belfastman but the Celtic elements (*leanbhan sí*—fairy child) and the bog-wood fire suggest the western location.

> Where Lagan stream sings lullaby,
>   There blows a lily fair.
> The twilight is in her eye,
>   The night is on her hair.
> And, like a lovesick leananshee,
>   She hath my heart in thrall.
> Nor life I own, nor liberty,
>   For love is lord of all.
>
> And often when the beetle's horn
>   Hath lulled the eve to sleep;
> I steal unto her shieling lorn,
>   And thro' the dooring peep.
> There in the crickets' singing-stone
>   She stirs the bogwood fire,
> And hums in sad sweet undertone,
>   The song of heart's desire.
>
> Her welcome, like her love for me,
>   Is from the heart within;
> Her warm kiss is felicity,
>   That knows no taint or sin,
> When she was only fairly small
>   Her gentle mother died,
> But true love keeps her memory warm
>   By Lagan's silver side.

She Moved Through the Fair

Padraic Colum

Another great feis and concert piece so well known and so often sung that it is incorrectly regarded as traditional.

My young love said to me, "My brothers won't mind,
And my parents won't slight you for your lack of kind."
Then she stepped away from me, and this she did say
"It will not be long, love, till our wedding day."

She stepped away from me and she moved through the fair,
And fondly I watched her go here and go there,
Then she went her way homeward with one star awake,
As the swan in the evening moves over the lake.

The people were saying no two were e'er wed
But one had a sorrow that never was said,
And I smiled as she passed with her goods and her gear,
And that was the last that I saw of my dear.

I dreamt it last night that my young love came in,
So softly she entered, her feet made no din;
She came close beside me, and this she did say
"It will not be long, love, till our wedding day."

If I Was a Blackbird

Anonymous

Street song, strong, melodic and instantly appealing.

Chorus
If I was a blackbird, I'd whistle and sing
And I'd follow the ship that my true love sails in,
And on the top rigging I'd there build my nest,
And I'd pillow my head on his lily white breast.

I am a young maiden and my story is sad
For once I was courted by a brave sailor lad.
He courted me strongly by night and by day,
But now my dear sailor is gone far away.

Chorus

He promised to take me to Donnybrook fair
To buy me red ribbons to bind up my hair.
And when he'd return from the ocean so wide,
He'd take me and make me his own loving bride.

Chorus

His parents they slight me and will not agree
That I and my sailor boy married should be.
But when he comes home I will greet him with joy
And I'll take to my bosom my dear sailor boy.

Chorus

The Planter's Daughter

Austin Clarke

Clarke at his assonantal best—a very delicate love poem.

When night stirred at sea
And the fire brought a crowd in,
They say that her beauty
Was music in mouth
And few in the candlelight
Thought her too proud,
For the house of the planter
Is known by the trees.

Men that had seen her
Drank deep and were silent,
The women were speaking
Wherever she went—
As a bell that is rung
Or a wonder told shyly,
And O she was the Sunday
In every week.

The Rose of Mooncoin

Seamus Kavanagh

A song which seemed fated to endless recurrence of popularity
but was at its height in the forties.

How sweet 'tis to roam by the sunny Suir stream
And hear the dove coo, neath the morning sun beam
Where the thrush and the robin their sweet notes entwine
On the banks of the Suir that flows down by Mooncoin.

Chorus

Flow on lovely river, flow gently along,
By your waters so clear sounds the lark's merry song,
On your green banks I'll wander where first I did join
With you, lovely Molly, the Rose of Mooncoin.

Oh! Molly, dear Molly, it breaks my fond heart.
To know that we two for ever must part.
I'll think of you Molly, while sun and moon shine.
On the banks of the Suir that flows down by Mooncoin.

Chorus

She sailed far away o'er the dark rolling foam,
Far away from the hills of her dear Irish home,
Where the fisherman sports with his small boat and line
By the banks of the Suir that flows down by Mooncoin.

Chorus

Then here's to the Suir with its valleys so fair,
As oftimes we wandered in the cool morning air,
Where the roses are blooming and lilies entwine
On the banks of the Suir that flows down by Mooncoin.

Chorus

VII
Irish Humour, Wet and Dry

Aqua Vitae

Richard Stanihurst

A great paean to the Water of Life as whiskey was also known in modern Irish. Stanihurst and Theoricus discovered many therapeutic virtues in the stuff and there are many in the country who are glad to assent.

THE SOILE OF IRELAND IS very low and waterish, including diverse little islands, invironed with lakes and marrish. Highest hills have standing pooles in their tops. Inhabitants especially new come, are subject to distillations, rheumes and fleures. For remedie whereof, they use an ordinarie drinke of *Aqua Vitae*, being so qualified in the making, that it drieth more and also inflameth lesse than other hot confections doo.

¶One *Theoricus* wrote a proper treatise of *Aqua Vitae* wherein he praiseth it unto the ninth degree. He distinguisheth three sorts thereof, *simplex, composita & perfectissima*. He declareth the simples and ingredients thereto belonging. He wisheth it to be taken as well before meat as after. It drieth up the breaking out of hands, & killeth the flesh wormes, if you wash your hands therewith. It scowreth all scurfe and scalds from the head, being therewith dailie washt before meales.

¶Being moderatlie taken, *saith he*, it sloweth age, it strengthneth youth, it helpeth digestion, it cutteth flegme, it abandoneth melancholie, it relisheth the heart, it lighteneth the mind, it quickeneth the spirits, it cureth the hydropsie, it healeth the strangurie, it pounceth the stone, it expelleth grauell, it puffeth away all ventositie, it keepeth and preserueth

the head from whirling, the eies from dazeling, the toong
from lisping, the mouth from maffling, the teeth from chatter-
ing, and the throte from ratling; it keepeth the weasan from
stifling, the stomach from wambling, and the heart from
swelling, the bellie from wirtching, the guts from rumbling,
the hands from shivering and the sinewes from shrinking, the
veines from crumpling, the bones from aking & the marrow
from soaking.

¶Vistadius also ascribeth thereto a singular praise, and would
have it to burne being kindled, which he taketh to be a token
to know the goodness thereof.

And trulie it is a sovereigne liquor, if it be orderlie taken.

from A Modest Proposal

Jonathan Swift

An excerpt from one of the finest, driest, bitterest pieces of sustained satire in English. Its effect was incalculable.

I have been assured by a very knowing American of my acquaintance in London, that a young healthy child well nursed is at a year old a most delicious, nourishing and wholesome food, whether stewed, roasted, baked, or boiled, and I make no doubt that it will equally serve in a *fricassée* or a *ragoût*.

I do therefore humbly offer it to public consideration, that of the hundred and twenty thousand children, already computed, twenty thousand may be reserved for breed, whereof only one-fourth part to be males, which is more than we allow to sheep, black cattle, or swine, and my reason is that these children are seldom the fruits of marriage, a circumstance not much regarded by our savages, therefore one male will be sufficient to serve four females. That the remaining hundred thousand may at a year old be offered in sale to the persons of quality, and fortune, through the kingdom, always advising the mother to let them suck plentifully in the last month, so as to render them plump and fat for a good table. A child will make two dishes at an entertainment for friends, and when the family dines alone, the fore or hind quarter will make a reasonable dish, and seasoned with a little pepper or salt will be very good boiled on the fourth day, especially in winter.

I have reckoned upon a medium, that a child just born will weigh twelve pounds, and in a solar year if tolerably nursed increaseth to twenty-eight pounds.

I grant this food will be somewhat dear, and therefore very proper for landlords, who, as they have already devoured most of the parents, seem to have the best title to the children.

Infant's flesh will be in season throughout the year, but more plentiful in March, and a little before and after, for we are told by a grave author, an eminent French physician, that fish being a prolific diet, there are more children born in Roman Catholic countries about nine months after Lent, than at any other season: therefore reckoning a year after Lent, the markets will be more glutted than usual, because the number of popish infants is at least three to one in this kingdom, and therefore it will have one other collateral advantage by lessening the number of papists among us.

I have already computed the charge of nursing a beggar's child (in which list I reckon all cottagers, labourers and four-fifths of the farmers) to be about two shillings *per annum*, rags included, and I believe no gentleman would repine to give ten shillings for the carcase of a good fat child, which, as I have said will make four dishes of excellent nutritive meat, when he hath only some particular friend, or his own family to dine with him. Thus the squire will learn to be a good landlord, and grow popular among his tenants, the mother will have eight shillings net profit, and be fit for work till she produces another child.

Those who are more thrifty (as I must confess the times require) may flay the carcase; the skin of which, artificially dressed, will make admirable gloves for ladies, and summer boots for fine gentlemen.

As to our City of Dublin, shambles may be appointed for this purpose, in the most convenient parts of it, and butchers we may be assured will not be wanting, although I rather recommend buying the children alive, and dressing them hot from the knife, as we do roasting pigs.

Johnny, I Hardly Knew Ye

Anonymous

The original savage version of the emasculate, "When Johnny
Comes Marching Home". "An eyeless, noseless, chickenless
egg" is as finely horrible a line as any in English.

While going the road to sweet Athy,
     Hurroo! hurroo!
While going the road to sweet Athy,
     Hurroo! hurroo!
While going the road to sweet Athy,
A stick in my hand and a drop in my eye,
A doleful damsel I heard cry:
"Och, Johnny, I hardly knew ye!
With drums and guns, and guns and drums
The enemy nearly slew ye;
My darling dear, you look so queer,
Och, Johnny, I hardly knew ye!

"Where are your eyes that looked so mild?
     Hurroo! hurroo!
Where are your eyes that looked so mild?
     Hurroo! hurroo!
Where are your eyes that looked so mild,
When my poor heart you first beguiled?
Why did you run from me and the child?
Och, Johnny, I hardly knew ye!
With drums, etc.

"Where are the legs with which you run?
     Hurroo! hurroo!
Where are the legs with which you run?
     Hurroo! hurroo!
Where are the legs with which you run

When you went to carry a gun?
Indeed, your dancing days are done!
Och, Johnny, I hardly knew ye!
With drums, etc.

"It grieved my heart to see you sail,
        Hurroo! hurroo!
It grieved my heart to see you sail,
        Hurroo! hurroo!
It grieved my heart to see you sail,
Though from my heart you took leg-bail;
Like a cod you're doubled up head and tail.
Och, Johnny, I hardly knew ye!
With drums, etc.

"You haven't an arm and you haven't a leg,
        Hurroo! hurroo!
You haven't an arm and you haven't a leg,
        Hurroo! hurroo!
You haven't an arm and you haven't a leg,
You're an eyeless, noseless, chickenless egg;
You'll have to be put with a bowl to beg:
Och, Johnny, I hardly knew ye!
With drums, etc.

"I'm happy for to see you home,
        Hurroo! hurroo!
I'm happy for to see you home,
        Hurroo! hurroo!
I'm happy for to see you home,
All from the island of Sulloon,
So low in flesh, so high in bone;
Och, Johnny, I hardly knew ye!
With drums, etc.

"But sad as it is to see you so,
   Hurroo, hurroo!
But sad as it is to see you so,
   Hurroo! hurroo!
But sad as it is to see you so,
And to think of you now as an object of woe,
Your Peggy'll still keep ye on as her beau;
Och, Johnny, I hardly knew ye!
With drums and guns, and guns and drums
The enemy nearly slew ye;
My darling dear, you look so queer,
Och, Johnny, I hardly knew ye!"

Stanzas on Women

(*from* The Vicar of Wakefield)

Oliver Goldsmith

Not really a verse from a male chauvinist chaplet but a finely ironic, pro-feminine comment from a partisan of the sex.

When lovely woman stoops to folly,
    And finds too late that men betray,
What charm can soothe her melancholy,
    What art can wash her guilt away?

The only art her guilt to cover,
    To hide her shame from every eye,
To give repentance to her lover,
    And wring his bosom, is—to die.

The Friar of Orders Gray

John O'Keefe

A jolly bass solo from O'Keefe's comic opera *Merry Sherwood*.

I am a friar of orders gray:
As down the valley I take my way,
 I pull not blackberry, haw, or hip,
 Good store of venison does fill my scrip:
My long bead-roll I merrily chaunt,
Where'er I walk, no money I want;
And why I'm so plump the reason I'll tell—
Who leads a good life is sure to live well.
  What baron or squire
  Or knight of the shire
 Lives half so well as a holy friar!

After supper, of heaven I dream,
But that is fat pullet and clouted cream.
 Myself, by denial, I mortify
 With a dainty bit of a warden pie:
I'm clothed in sackcloth for my sin:
With old sack wine I'm lined within:
A chirping cup is my matin song,
And the vesper bell is my bowl's ding dong.
  What baron or squire
  Or knight of the shire
 Lives half so well as a holy friar!

Let the Toast Pass

(*from* The School for Scandal)

Richard Brinsley Sheridan

Sheridan was the leading eighteenth-century dramatist in one
of the regularly recurring periods when it fell to the Irish to
teach the English how to write plays. The word "quean" in
line 3 means "whore" and not "our own dear. . ."

Here's to the maiden of bashful fifteen,
Here's to the widow of fifty
Here's to the flaunting extravagant quean
And here's to the housewife that's thrifty.

Chorus
Let the toast pass,
Drink to the lass,
I'll warrant she'll prove an excuse for the glass.

Here's to the charmer, whose dimples we prize,
Now to the maid who has none, sir,
Here's to the girl with a pair of blue eyes,
And here's to the nymph with but one, sir.

Chorus

Here's to the maid with a bosom of snow,
And to her that's as brown as a berry;
Here's to the wife, with a face full of woe,
And now to the girl that is merry.

Chorus

For let 'em be clumsy, or let 'em be slim,
Young or ancient, I care not a feather;
So fill the pint bumper, quite up to the brim,
And let us all toast them together.

Chorus

Sir Boyle Roche

Sir Jonah Barrington

One smart flamboyant Anglo-Irishman writing about one
considerably less smart.

I will now advert to Sir Boyle Roche, who certainly was,
without exception, the most celebrated and entertaining
anti-grammarian in the Irish Parliament. I knew him inti-
mately. He was of a very respectable Irish family, and in point
of appearance, a fine, bluff, soldier-like old gentleman. He
had numerous good qualities; and, having been long in the
army, his ideas were full of honour and etiquette—of discipline
and bravery. He had a claim to the title of Fermoy, which,
however, he never pursued; and was brother to the famous
Tiger Roche, who fought some desperate duel abroad, and
was near being hanged for it. Sir Boyle was perfectly well-
bred in all his habits; had been appointed gentleman-usher at
the Irish court, and executed the duties of that office to the
day of his death, with the utmost satisfaction to himself, as
well as to everyone in connection with him. He was married
to the eldest daughter of Sir John Cave, Bart; and his lady,
who was a "bas bleu" prematurely injured Sir Boyle's capacity
(it was said) by forcing him to read Gibbon's *Rise and Fall of
the Roman Empire* whereat he was so cruelly puzzled without
being in the least amused, that in his cups he often stigmatised
the great historian as a low fellow, who ought to have been
kicked out of company wherever he was, for turning people's
thoughts away from their prayers and their politics to what
the devil himself could make neither head nor tail of.

His perpetually bragging that Sir John Cave had given him
his *eldest* daughter, afforded Curran an opportunity of reply-
ing, "Ay, Sir Boyle, and depend on it, if he had an *older* one

still he would have given her to you." Sir Boyle thought it best to receive the repartee as a compliment, lest it should come to her ladyship's ears, who, for several years back, had prohibited Sir Boyle from all allusions to chronology.

The baronet had certainly one great advantage over all other bull and blunder makers: he seldom launched a blunder from which some fine aphorism or maxim might not be easily extracted. When a debate arose in the Irish House of Commons on the vote of a grant which was recommended by Sir John Parnell, Chancellor of the Exchequer, as one not likely to be felt burdensome for many years to come—it was observed in reply, that the House had no just right to load posterity with a weighty debt for what could in no degree operate to their advantage. Sir Boyle, eager to defend the measure of Government, immediately rose, and in a very few words, put forward the most unanswerable argument which human ingenuity could possibly devise. "What, Mr. Speaker!" said he, "and so we are to beggar ourselves for fear of vexing posterity! Now, I would ask the honourable gentleman, and *still more* honourable House, why we should put ourselves out of our way to do anything for *posterity;* for what has *posterity* done for *us?*"

Sir Boyle, hearing the roar of laughter, which of course followed this sensible blunder, but not being conscious that he had said anything out of the way, was rather puzzled, and conceived that the House had misunderstood him. He therefore begged leave to explain, as he apprehended that gentleman had entirely mistaken his words: he assured the House that "by *posterity,* he did not at all mean *our ancestors,* but those who were to come *immediately* after *them.*" Upon hearing this *explanation,* it was impossible to do any serious business for half an hour.

Sir Boyle was induced by Government to fight as hard as possible for the Union; so he did, and I really believe fancied, by degrees, that he was right. On one occasion, a general titter arose at his florid picture of the happiness which must proceed from this event. "Gentlemen," said Sir Boyle, "may titther, and titther, and titther, and may think it a bad measure; but their heads at present are hot, and will remain so till they grow cool again; and so they can't decide right now; but when the *day of judgment* comes, *then* honourable gentlemen will be satisfied at this most excellent union. Sir, there is no Levitical degree between nations, and on this occasion I can see neither sin nor shame in *marrying our own sister.*"

He was a determined enemy to the French Revolution, and seldom rose in the House for several years without volunteering some abuse of it. "Mr. Speaker," said he, in a mood of this kind, "if we once permitted the villainous French masons to meddle with the buttresses and walls of our ancient constitution, they would never stop, nor stay, sir, till they brought the foundation-stones tumbling down about the ears of the nation! There," continued Sir Boyle, placing his hand earnestly on his heart, his powdered head shaking in unison with his loyal zeal, while he described the probable consequences of an invasion of Ireland by the French republicans; "there, Mr. Speaker! if those Gallican villains should invade us, sir, 'tis on *that very table*, maybe, these honourable members might see their own destinies lying in heaps on top of one another! Here perhaps, sir, the murderous Marshal-law-men (Marseillais) would break in, cut us to mince-meat and throw our bleeding heads upon that table to stare us in the face!"

The Finding of Moses

Zozimus

Zozimus was the last of the gleemen. Blind from an early age, he wrote songs and ballads which he sold from his stand on Carlisle (now O'Connell) Bridge. His versions of biblical and other historical events rendered for Howth Castle and Environs were very popular.

On Egypt's banks, contagious to the Nile
The Ould Pharoah's daughter, she went to bathe in style.
She took her dip and she came unto the land,
And to dry her royal pelt she ran along the strand.
A bullrush tripped her whereupon she saw
A smiling baby in a wad of straw;
She took him up and says she in accents mild
"Oh taranagers, girls, now, which of yis owns the child?"

She took him up and she gave a little grin
For she and Moses were standing in their skin,
"Bedad now" says she "It was someone very rude
Left a little baby by the river in his nude."
She took him to her oul lad sitting on the throne
"Da," says she, "Will you give the boy a home?"
"Bedad now," says he, "Sure I've often brought in worse.
Go my darlin daughter and get the child a nurse."

An oul blackamore woman among the crew
Cried out "You royal savage, what's that to do with you?
Your royal ladies is too meek and mild
To beget dishonestly this darling little child."
"Ah then," says Pharoah, "I'll search every nook
From the Phoenix Park down to Donnybrook
And when I catch hoult of the bastard's father
I will kick him from the Nile down to the Dodder."

Well they sent a bellman to the Market Square
To see if he could find a slavey there
But the only one now that he could find
Was the little young one that left the child behind.
She came up to Pharoah, a stranger, mareyah,
Never lettin on that she was the baby's ma.
And so little Moses got his mammy back
Shows that co-in-ci-dence is a nut to crack.

The Agricultural Irish Girl

Anonymous

A low but genuine (presumably male) tribute to an almost
extinct national type.

If all the women in the town were bundled up together,
I know a girl could beat them all, in any kind of weather;
The rain can't wash the powder off, because she does not
      wear it,
Her face and figure's all her own: it's true, for I declare it!

Chorus
For she's a big stout, strong lump of an agricultural Irish girl,
She neither paints nor powders and her figure is all her own,
And she can strike that hard that you'd think that you'd
      been struck by the kick of a mule,
It's "the full of the house" of Irish love is Mary Ann
      Malone.

She was only seventeen last grass, and still improving
      greatly;
I wonder what she'll be at all when her bones are set
      completely,
You'd think your hand was in a vice the moment that she
      shakes it.
And if there's any cake around, it's Mary Ann that takes it.

Chorus

Coortin' in the Kitchen

Anonymous

Famous Dublin song and cautionary tale with several more modern and etiolated versions.

Come single belle and beau to me now pay attention,
And love I'll plainly show is the divil's own invention,
For once in love I fell, with a maiden's smiles bewitching,
Miss Henrietta Bell down in Captain Phibb's kitchen.

Chorus
Ri tooral ooral lah ri tooral ooral addy
Ri tooral ooral lah ri tooral ooral addy

At the age of seventeen I was tied unto a grocer,
Not far from Stephen's Green, where Miss Bell for tea
      would go, sir.
Her manners were so free, she set my heart a-twitching,
She invited me to tea, down in Captain Phibbs's kitchen.

Next Sunday being the day, we were to have the flare-up,
I dressed myself quite gay, an' I frizz'd and oiled my hair
      up.
As the captain had no wife, he had gone out a-fishin',
So we kicked up high life, below-stairs in the kitchen.

Just as the clock struck six we sat down to the table;
She handed tea and cakes—I ate while I was able.
I ate cakes, drank punch and tea, till my side had got a
      stitch in,
And the hours flew quick away, while coortin' in the
      kitchen.

With my arms round her waist I kissed—she hinted
    marriage—
To the door in dreadful haste came Captain Phibbs's
    carriage.
Her looks told me full well, that moment she was wishin'
That I'd get out to H—, or somewhere far from the
    kitchen.

She flew up off my knees, full five feet up or higher,
And over head and heels, threw me slap into the fire.
My new Repealer's coat, that I bought from Mr. Stitchen
With a thirty-shilling note, went to blazes in the kitchen.

I grieved to see my duds, all besmeared with smoke and
    ashes,
When a tub of dirty suds, right in my face she dashes.
As I lay on the floor still the water she kept pitchin',
Till the footman broke the door, and marched down into
    the kitchen.

When the captain came down stairs, though he seen my
    situation,
In spite of all my prayers I was marched off to the station.
For me they'd take no bail, tho' to get home I was itchin',
But I had to tell the tale, of how I came into the kitchen.

I said she did invite me, but she gave a flat denial,
For assault she did indict me, and I was sent for trial.
She swore I robbed the house in spite of her screechin'.
So I six months went round the rack for coortin' in the
    kitchen.

The Cruiskeen Lawn

Anonymous

A late eighteeth-century tributė to the full-jug whose hidden
Irish words mean:
"Love of my heart, my little jug;
Bright health to my sweetheart;
Love of my heart my fair-haired girl."

Let the farmer praise his grounds,
Let the huntsman praise his hounds,
　　The shepherd his dew-scented lawn;
But I, more blest than they,
Spend each happy night and day
　　With my charming little cruiskeen lawn, lawn, lawn,
　　My charming little cruiskeen lawn.
　　　　Gra ma chree ma cruiskeen,
　　　　Slainte geal mavourneen,
　　　　Gra machree a coolin bawn.

　　　　Gra machree ma cruiskeen,
　　　　Slainte geal mavourneen,
　　　　Gra machree a coolin bawn, bawn, bawn,
　　　　Gra machree a coolin bawn.

Immortal and divine,
Great Bacchus, god of wine,
　　Create me by adoption your son:
In hope that you'll comply
My glass shall ne'er run dry,
　　Nor my smiling little cruiskeen lawn, &c.

And when grim death appears,
In a few but pleasant years,

To tell me that my glass has run;
I'll, say, Begone, you knave,
For bold Bacchus gave me leave,
  To take another cruiskeen lawn, &c.

Then fill your glasses high,
Let's not part with lips a-dry.
  Though the lark now proclaims it is dawn;
And since we can't remain,
May we shortly meet again,
  To fill another cruiskeen lawn, lawn, lawn,
  To fill another cruiskeen lawn.
    Gra ma chree ma cruiskeen,
    Slainte geal mavourneen,
    Gra machree a coolin bawn.

    Gra ma chree ma cruiskeen,
    Slainte geal mavourneen,
    Gra machree a coolin bawn, bawn, bawn,
    Gra machree a coolin bawn.

I Don't Mind If I Do

Anonymous

An Irish "softie" song, the national equivalent of "Willikens and his Dinah".

Now you asked me to sing you a bit of a song,
Tis not very short and it's not very long,
You asked me to sing about something that's new,
"Be-dad, now," says I "I don't mind if I do."

Well my name 'tis Dan Murphy and a farmer am I,
I courted a lass and I felt rather shy,
She invited me in for a moment or two,
"Be-dad, now", say I, "I don't mind if I do."

When we entered the kitchen it was cozy, and bright,
Soon a fine hearty supper I put out of sight,
Says she, "Would you care for one glass or two?"
"Be-dad, now," say I, "I don't mind if I do."

When the supper was finished, I reached for my hat,
Said Peggy, the darling, "Don't leave me like that,
Now wouldn't you care for just one kiss or two?"
"Be-dad, now," says I, "I don't mind if I do."

So we talked about that and we talked about this,
Bearing the time she was stealing a kiss,
"Do you love me?" asked Peggy, "For I do love you"
"Be-dad now," says I, "I don't mind if I do."

So we hugged and we squeezed in fond lover's delight,
Said Peggy, the darling, "Please make me your wife,
I've an acre of ground and I've one cow or two,"
"Be-dad now," says I, "I don't mind if I do."

We went the next morning to the Church to be wed.
The preacher presented the book and he said,
"Now let you take Peggy and Peggy 'll take you,"
"Be-dad now," says I, "I don't mind if I do."

Twelve months we've been married and we've one little lad,
The neighbours do swear that he's just like his dad,
But Peggy wants more, at least one or two,
"Be-dad, now," says I, "I don't mind if I do."

Let Him Go, Let Him Tarry

Anonymous

Dismissal song for female singer, very spirited.

Farewell to cold winter, summer's come at last,
Nothing have I gained, but my true love I have lost.
I'll sing and I'll be happy like the birds upon the tree,
But since he deceived me I care no more for he.

Chorus
Let him go, let him tarry,
Let him sink or let him swim,
He doesn't care for me nor I don't care for him,
He can go and get another, that I hope he will enjoy,
For I'm going to marry a far nicer boy.

He wrote me a letter saying he was very bad,
I sent him back an answer saying I was awful glad.
He wrote to me another saying he was well and strong,
But I care no more about him than the ground he walks
      upon.

Chorus

Some of his friends they had a very good kind wish for me,
Other of his friends, they could hang me on a tree;
But soon I'll let them see my love and soon I'll let them
      know
That I can get a new sweetheart on any ground I go.

Chorus

He can go to his old mother now, and set her mind at ease,
I hear she is an old, old woman, very hard to please.
It's slighting me and talking ill is what she's always done.
Because that I was courting her great big ugly son.

Chorus

The Maid of the Sweet Brown Knowe

Anonymous

Dismissal song for male singer, equally spirited.

Come all ye lads and lasses and hear my mournful tale,
Ye tender hearts that weep for love to sigh you will not fail,
'Tis all about a young man and my song will tell you how
He lately came a-courting of the Maid of the Sweet Brown
     Knowe.

Said he, "My pretty fair maid, could you and I agree,
To join our hands in wedlock bands, and married we will
     be;
We'll join our hands in wedlock bands, and you'll have my
     plighted vow,
That I'll do my whole endeavours for the Maid of the Sweet
     Brown Knowe."

Now this young and pretty fickle thing, she knew not what
     to say,
Her eyes did shine like silver bright and merrily did play;
Says she, "Young man, your love subdue, I am not ready
     now,
And I'll spend another season at the foot of the Sweet
     Brown Knowe."

"Oh," says he, "My pretty fair maid, now why do you say
     so?
Look down in yonder valley where my verdant crops do
     grow
Look down in yonder valley at my horses and my plough
All at their daily labour for the Maid of the Sweet Brown
     Knowe."

"If they're at their daily labour, kind sir, it is not for me.
I've heard of your behaviour, I have, kind sir," says she;
"There is an inn where you drop in, I've heard the people
      say,
Where you rap and you call and you pay for all, and go
      home at the dawn of day."

"If I rap and I call and I pay for all, my money is all my
      own,
I've never spent aught o' your fortune, for I hear that
      you've got none.
You thought you had my poor heart broke in talking to me
      now,
But I'll leave you where I found you, at the foot of the
      Sweet Brown Knowe."

The Old Orange Flute

Anonymous

The best of the Orange comic songs, too self-mocking to have been written by a hardliner and probably sung with greater frequency and gusto by Papishes anyway.

In the County Tyrone, in the town of Dungannon,
Where many a ruction myself had a han' in.
Bob Williamson lived, a weaver by trade
And all of us thought him a stout Orange blade,
On the Twelfth of July as around it would come
Bob played on the flute to the sound of the drum,
You may talk of your harp, your piano or lute
But there's nothing compared with the Ould Orange flute.

But Bob the deceiver he took us all in,
For he married a Papish called Brigid McGinn,
Turned Papish himself, and forsook the old cause
That gave us our freedom, religion, and laws.
Now the boys of the place made some comment upon it,
And Bob had to fly to the Province of Connacht
He fled with his wife and his fixings to boot,
And along with the latter his old Orange flute.

At the chapel on Sundays, to atone for past deeds,
He said *Paters* and *Aves* and counted his beads,
Till after some time, at the priest's own desire,
He went with his old flute to play in the choir.
He went with his old flute to play for the Mass,
And the instrument shivered, and sighed: "Oh, alas!"
And blow as he would, though it made a great noise.
The flute would play only "The Protestant Boys."

Bob jumped, and he started, and got in a flutter,
And threw his old flute in the blest Holy Water;
He thought that this charm would bring some other sound
When he blew it again, it played "Croppies lie down";
And for all he could whistle, and finger, and blow,
To play Papish music he found it no go;
"Kick the Pope," "The Boyne Water," it freely would
     sound,
But one Papish squeak in it couldn't be found.

At a council of priests that was held the next day,
They decided to banish the old flute away
For they couldn't knock heresy out of its head
And they bought Bob a new one to play in its stead.
So the old flute was doomed and its fate was pathetic,
'Twas fastened and burned at the stake as heretic,
While the flames roared around it they heard a strange
     noise—
'Twas the old flute still whistling "The Protestant Boys."

There's Whiskey in the Jar

Anonymous

A highwayman song and very popular with the Fancy and in the mainstream (if that's the word) of Ireland's bibulous choral tradition.

As I was going over the far famed Kerry mountain
I met with Captain Farrell and his money he was counting
I first produced my pistol and then produced my rapier
Sayin', "Stand and deliver for you are my bold deceiver,"
O, whack fol the diddle, O, whack fol the diddle, O,
There's whiskey in the jar
Whack fol the diddle, O, whack fol the diddle, O,
There's whiskey in the jar.

He counted out his money and it made a pretty penny
I put it in my pocket and I gave it to my Jenny
She sighed and she swore that she never would betray me
But the devil take the women for they never can be easy.

I went unto my chamber all for to take a slumber
I dreamt of gold and jewels and for sure it was no wonder
But Jenny drew my charges and she filled them up with
    water
An' she sent for Captain Farrell, to be ready for the
    slaughter.

And 'twas early in the morning before I rose to travel,
Up comes a band of footmen and likewise Captain Farrell;
I then produced my pistol, for she stole away my rapier
But I couldn't shoot the water so a prisoner I was taken.

And if any one can aid me 'tis my brother in the army
If I could learn his station, in Cork or in Killarney.
And if he'd come and join me we'd go-roving in Kilkenny
I'll engage he'd treat me fairer than my darling sporting
　　　　Jenny.

Tim Finnigan's Wake

Anonymous

Joyce's social education had a strong element of song in it. Not only was he a sterling performer himself but he was reared in full acquaintance of opera and operetta and also of the rich Irish ballad tradition. This jolly song with its elements of resurrection from the dead was an obvious seed for his great dream.

Tim Finnigan lived in Walker street,
A gentleman Irishman—mighty odd—
He'd a beautiful brogue, so rich and sweet,
And to rise in the world, he carried the hod.
But, you see he'd a sort of a tippling way;
With a love for the liquor poor Tim was born,
And to help him through his work, each day,
He'd a drop of the creatur' every morn.

Chorus
Whack; hurrah! blood and 'ounds! ye sowl ye,
Welt the flure, yer trothers shake,
Isn't it the truth I've tould ye?
Lots of fun at Finnigan's wake?

One morning, Tim was rather full;
His head felt heavy, which made him shake,
He fell from the ladder, and broke his skull,
So they carried him home a corpse to wake.
They rolled him up in a nice clean sheet,
And laid him out upon the bed,
With fourteen candles around his feet,
And a couple of dozen around his head.

Chorus

His friends assembled at his wake;
Missus Finnigan called out for the lunch.
First they laid in tea and cake;
Then pipes and tobacky and whiskey-punch,
Miss Biddy O'Brien began to cry;
"Such a pretty corpse did ever you see?
Arrah! Tim avourneen, an' why did ye die?"
"Och, none of your gab," sez Judy Magee.

Chorus

Then Peggy O'Connor took up the job,
"Arrah! Biddy," says she, "ye're wrong, I'm shure,"
But Judy then gave her a belt on the gob,
And left her sprawling on the flure.
Each side in war did soon engage,
'Twas woman to woman and man to man,
Shillelah-law was all the rage—
An' a bloody ruction soon began.

Chorus

Mickey Mulvaney raised his head.
When a gallon of whiskey flew at him.
It missed him—and hopping on the bed,
The liquor scattered over Tim!
Bedad he revives! see how he raises!
An' Timothy, jumping from the bed,
Cries, while he lathered around like blazes:
"Bad luck to yer sowls! d'ye think I'm dead?"

Chorus

The Women are Worse than the Men

Anonymous

A ballad usually known as "Killyburn Brae", whose Ulster provenance is seen in the Scots dialect words. It traduces womenkind with splendid lack of justice.

Is it true that the women are worse than the men
Right fol right fol tiddy fol lay

Is it true that the women are worse than the men,
That they went down to Hell and were thrown out again,

With your right fol lol tiddy fol lol
Fol the dol lol the lol, lol the dol lay.

Now there was an old man lived at Killyburn braes
And he had a wife was the plague of his days.

The divil he came to the man at the plough,
Saying, "One of your family I must take now."

Said he, "My good man, I've come for your wife,
For I hear she's the plague and torment of your life."

So the divil he hoisted her up on his back,
And landed at Hell's hall-door with a crack.

There were two little divils a playing with chains,
She upp'd with her stick, and knocked out their brains.

There were two other divils looked over the wall
They said, "Take her away or she'll murder us all."

So the divil he hoisted her up on his back,
And back to the old man hurried the pack.

They were seven years going and nine coming back,
Yet she asked for the scrapings she left in the pot.

Said he, "My good man, here's your wife back again,
For she wouldn't be kept, not even in Hell!

Now, I've been a divil the most of my life.
But I ne'er was in Hell till I met with your wife."

So it's true that the women are worse than the men,
For they went down to Hell and were threw out again.

Father O'Flynn

A. P. Graves

Graves's most famous song which because of a faint but stingless suggestion of stage-Irishism tends to enrage the unco-guid and ultra-nationalist. Cannot the Irish have gaiety too?

Of priests we can offer a charmin' variety,
Far renowned for larnin' and piety;
Still, I'd advance you, widout impropriety,
　　Father O'Flynn as the flower of them all.

Chorus
Here's a health to you, Father O'Flynn,
Slainte, and slainte, and slainte agin'
　　Powerfulest preacher, and
　　Tinderest teacher, and
Kindliest creature in ould Donegal.

Don't talk of your Provost and Fellows of Trinity,
Famous for ever at Greek and Latinity
Dad and the divels and all at Divinity,
　　Father O'Flynn 'd makes hares of them all.
　　　Come, I vinture to give you my word,
　　　Never the likes of his logic was heard
　　　　Down from Mythology
　　　　Into Thayology.
　　　Troth, and Conchology, if he'd the call.

Chorus

Och, Father O'Flynn, you've the wonderful way wid you
All ould sinners are wishful to pray wid you,

All the young childer are wild for to play wid you,
   You've such a way wid you, Father avick,
Still, for all you've so gentle a soul,
     Gad, you've your flock in the grandest conthroul:
      Checking the crazy ones,
     Liftin' the lazy ones, on wid the stick.

Chorus

And though quite avoidin' all foolish frivolity
Still at all seasons of innocent jollity,
Where was the play-boy could claim an equality
   At comicality, Father, wid you?
     Once the Bishop looked grave at your jest,
     Till this remark sent him off wid the rest,
      "Is it the gaiety
      All to the laity?
     Cannot the clargy be Irishmen too?"

Chorus

Phil the Fluther's Ball

Percy French

French's record of imperishable songs is enviable and daunting and this is one of his most famous. To the begrudgers it must be said the character was genuine, a Leitrim tenant farmer who told the Rev. Mr. Godley, a friend of French's, that whenever he was short for the rent money he "giv a ball". "I put me hat behind the door, the neighbours come in, bringing their suppers with them, and each puttin' a shillin' or two in the hat. I cock me leg over the dresser, throw me lip over the flute and toother away like a hat full of larks and there they stay leppin' like hares till two in the mornin'."

Have you heard of Phil the Fluther, of the town of
    Ballymuck?
The times were going hard with him, in fact the man was
    bruk',
So he just sent out a notice to his neighbours, one and all,
As how he'd like their company that ev'ning at a ball.
And when writin' out he was careful to suggest to them,
That if they found a hat of his convaniant to the dure,
The more they put in, whenever he requested them,
"The better would the music be for battherin' the flure."

Chorus
With the toot of the flute,
And the twiddle of the fiddle, O'
Hopping in the middle, like a herrin' on a griddle, O'
Up, down, hands a-rown'
Crossin' to the wall,
Oh! hadn't we the gaiety at Phil the Fluther's Ball!

There was Misther Denis Dogherty, who kep' "The
      Runnin' Dog";
There was little crooked Paddy from the Tiraloughett bog:
There were boys from every Barony, and girls from every
      "art,"
And the beautiful Miss Bradys, in a private ass an' cart.
And along with them came bouncing Mrs. Cafferty,
Little Micky Mulligan was also to the fore;
Rose, Suzanne, and Margaret O'Rafferty,
The flower of Ardmagullion, and the Pride of Pethravore.

Chorus

First little Micky Mulligan got up to show them how,
And then the widda' Cafferty steps out and makes her bow.
"I could dance you off your legs," sez she, "as sure as you
      are born,
If ye'll only make the piper play 'the hare was in the
      corn'."
So, Phil plays up to the best of his ability,
The lady and the gentleman begin to do their share;
Faith, then Mick, it's you that has agility!
Begorra! Mrs. Cafferty, yer leppin' like a hare!

Chorus

Then Phil the Fluther tipped a wink to little crooked Pat,
"I think it's nearly time," sez he, "for passin' round the
      hat."
So Paddy passed the caubeen round, and looking mighty
      cute,
Sez, "Ye've got to pay the piper when he toothers on the
      flute."
Then all joined in wid the greatest joviality,
Covering the buckle and the shuffle, and the cut;
Jigs were danced, of very finest quality,
But the Widda bet the company at "handeling the fut."

Shlathery's Mounted Fut

Percy French

French's not very subtle but essentially mild guying of the
drilling that went on North and South in the years of the
Home Rule agitation. As with most of French's work, the
humour is not entirely broad: neat spies of subtlety creep in
here and there among the slapstick.

You've heard o' Julius Caesar, an' the great Napoleon, too,
An' how the Cork Militia beat the Turks at Waterloo;
But there's a page of glory that, as yet, remains uncut,
An' that's the Martial story o' the Shlathery's Mounted Fut.
This gallant corps was organised by Shlathery's eldest son.
A noble-minded poacher, wid a double-breasted gun;
An' many a head was broken, aye, an' many an eye was
        shut,
Whin practisin' manoeuvres in the Shlathery's Mounted
        Fut.

Chorus
An' down from the mountains came the squadrons an'
        platoons,
Four-an'-twinty fightin' min, an' a couple o' sthout
        gossoons,
An' whin we marched behind the dhrum to patriotic tunes,
We felt that fame would gild the name o' Shlathery's Light
        Dhragoons.

Well, first we reconnoithered round o' O'Sullivan's
        Shebeen—
It used to be "The Shop House," but we call it, "The
        Canteen;"

272

But there we saw a notice which the bravest heart
        unnerved—
"All liquor must be settled for before the dhrink is served."
So on we marched, but soon again each warrior's heart
        grew pale,
For risin' high in front o' us we saw the County Jail;
An' whin the army faced about, 'twas just in time to find
A couple o' policemin had surrounded us behind.

Chorus
Still, from the mountains came the squadrons and platoons,
Four-an'-twinty fightin' min, an' a couple o' sthout
        gossoons;
Says Shlathery, "We must circumvent these bludgeonin'
        bosthoons,
Or else it sames they'll take the names o' Shlathery's Light
        Dhragoons.

"We'll cross the ditch," our leader cried, "an' take the foe
        in flank,"
But yells of consthernation here arose from every rank,
For posted high upon a tree we very plainly saw,
"Threspassers prosecuted, in accordance wid' the law."
"We're foiled!" exclaimed bowld Shlathery, "here ends our
        grand campaign,
'Tis merely throwin' life away to face that mearin' dhrain,
I'm not as bold as lions, but I'm braver nor a hin,
An' he that fights and runs away will live to fight agin."

Chorus
An' back to the mountains went the squadrons and
        platoons,
Four-an'-twinty fightin' min an' a couple o' sthout
        gossoons;
The band was playing cautiously their patriotic tunes;
To sing the fame, if rather lame o' Shlathery's Light
        Dhragoons.

The Curse

To a sister of an enemy of the author's who disapproved of
"The Playboy"

John Millington Synge

A fine piece of Synge invective with characteristic Jacobean
detail, each insult as fully flavoured as a nut or an apple. The
object of the attack was Mrs Callender, Molly Allgood's sister,
and this version is much milder than the original.

Lord, confound this surly sister,
Blight her brow with blotch and blister,
Cramp her larynx, lung, and liver,
In her guts a galling give her.

Let her live to earn her dinners
In Mountjoy with seedy sinners:
Lord, this judgment quickly bring,
And I'm Your servant, J. M. Synge.

The Liberator and Biddy Moriarty

Anonymous

One of several accounts of a battle of undeleted expletives between two of the great forensic exponents of the day.

There was at that time in Dublin, a certain woman, Biddy Moriarty, who had a huckster's stall on one of the quays nearly opposite the Four Courts. She was a virago of the first order, very able with her fist, and still more formidable with her tongue. From one end of Dublin to the other, she was notorious for her powers of abuse, and even in the provinces Mrs. Moriarty's language had passed into currency. The dictionary of Dublin slang had been considerably enlarged by her, and her voluble impudence had almost become proverbial. Some of O'Connell's friends, however, thought that he could beat her at the use of her own weapons. Of this, however, he had some doubts himself, when he listened once or twice to some minor specimens of her Billingsgate. It was mooted once where the young Kerry barrister could encounter her, and some one of the company rather too freely ridiculed the idea of his being able to meet the famous Madame Moriarty. O'Connell never liked the idea of being put down, and he professed his readiness to encounter her, and even backed himself for the match. Bets were offered and taken and it was decided that the matter should come off at once.

The party adjourned to the huckster's stall, and there was the owner herself, superintending the sale of her small wares — a few loungers and ragged idlers were hanging around her stall, for Biddy was a character and in her way was one of the sights of Dublin. O'Connell commenced the attack.

"What's the price of this walking-stick, Mrs. What's-your-name?"

"Moriarty, sir, is my name, and a good one it is; and what have you to say agen it? One-and-sixpence's the price of the stick. Troth, it's chape as dirt, so it is."

"One-and-sixpence for a walking stick; whew! why, you are not better than an imposter, to ask eighteen pence for what cost you two pence."

"Two pence, your grandmother! Do you mane to say it's chating the people I am? Imposter, indeed!"

"I protest as I am a gentleman. . ."

"Jintleman! Jintleman! The likes of you a jintleman! Wisha, by gor, that bangs Banagher. Why, you potato-faced pippin-sneezer, when did a Madagascar monkey like you pick up enough of common Christian dacency to hide your Kerry brogue?"

"Easy now, easy now," said O'Connell with imperturbable good humour, "don't choke yourself with fine language, you whiskey-drinking parallelogram."

"What's that you call me, you murderin' villain?" roared Mrs. Moriarty.

"I call you," answered O'Connell, "a parallelogram; and a Dublin judge and jury will say it's no libel to call you so."

"Oh, tare-an'-ouns! Oh, Holy Saint Bridget! that an honest woman like me should be called a parrybellygrum to her face. I'm none of your parrybellygrums, you rascally gallows-bird; you cowardly, sneakin', plate-lickin' blaguard!"

"Oh, not you, indeed! Why, I suppose you'll deny that you keep a hypotenuse in your house."

"It's a lie for you. I never had such a thing. . . ."

"Why, sure all your neighbours know very well that you keep not only a hypotenuse, but that you have two diameters locked up in your garret, and that you go out to walk with them every Sunday, you heartless old heptagon."

"Oh, hear that, ye saints in glory! Oh, there's bad language from a fellow that wants to pass for a jintleman. May the divil fly away with you, you micher from Munster, and make celery-sauce of your rotten limbs, you mealy-mouthed tub of guts."

"Ah, you can't deny the charge, you miserable sub-multiple of a duplicate ratio."

"Go, rinse your mouth in the Liffey, you nasty tickle-pincher; after all the bad words you speak, it ought to be dirtier than your face, you dirty chicken of Beelzebub."

"Rinse your own mouth, you wicked-minded old polygon—to the deuce I pitch you, you blustering intersection of a superficies!"

"You saucy tinker's apprentice, if you don't cease your jaw, I'll. . . ." But here she gasped for breath, unable to hawk up more words.

"While I have a tongue, I'll abuse you, you most inimitable periphery. Look at her, boys! There she stands—a convicted perpendicular in petticoats! There's contamination in her circumference, and she trembles with guilt down to the extremities of her corollaries. Ah, you're found out, you rectilineal-antecedent, and equiangular old hag! 'Tis with the devil you will fly away, you porter-swiping similitude of the bisection of a vortex!"

Overwhelmed with this torrent of language, Mrs. Moriarty was silenced. Catching up a saucepan, she was aiming at O'Connell's head, when he made a timely retreat.

"You've won your wager, O'Connell, here's your bet," said the ones who proposed the contest.

Whack Fol the Diddle

Peadar Kearney

Good-natured satire and as such rather more effective than
the usual Irish stuff on that account. Pieter's Hill was the site
of a battle in 1899 in the Second Boer War; Beal an Atha
Buidhe was the Battle of the Yellow Ford in 1598 where the
O'Neill defeated and killed Marshal Bagenal.

I sing you a song of peace and love,
Whack fol the diddle lol the di do day,
To the land that reigns all lands above,
Whack fol the diddle lol the di do day.
May peace and plenty be her share,
Who kept our homes from want and care,
Oh God bless England is our prayer,
Whack fol the diddle lol the di do day.

Chorus
Whack fol the diddle lol the di do day.
So we say Hip Hurrah!
Come and listen while we pray
Whack fol the diddle lol the di do day.

When we were savage, fierce and wild,
Whack fol the diddle lol the di do day.
She came as a mother to her child,
Whack fol the diddle lol the di do day.
Gently raised us from the slime,
Kept our hands from hellish crime,
And sent us to heaven in her own good time,
Whack fol the diddle lol the di do day.

Chorus

Our fathers oft' were naughty boys,
Whack fol the diddle lol the di do day.
Pikes and guns are dangerous toys,
Whack fol the diddle lol the di do day.
From Beal an Atha Buidhe to Pieters Hill
They made poor England weep her fill,
But old Britannia loves us still,
Whack fol the diddle lol the di do day.

Chorus

Oh Irishmen forget the past,
Whack fol the diddle lol the di do day,
And think of the day that is coming fast,
Whack fol the diddle lol the di do day.
When we shall all be civilized
Neat and clean and well advised,
Oh won't Mother England be surprised!
Whack fol the diddle lol the di do day.

The Ballad of William Bloat

Raymond Calvert

A modern folktale from Belfast, guaranteed Irish.

In a mean abode, on the Shankill Road,
Lived a man called William Bloat,
He had a wife, the curse of his life,
Who continually "got his goat".
So, one day at dawn, with her nightdress on—
He cut her b--- throat.

With a razor-gash, he settled her hash,
O' never was crime so quick;
But the steady drip, on the pillow-slip,
Of her life-blood made him sick,
And the pool of gore, on the bedroom floor,
Grew clotted, cold and thick.

And yet—he was glad that he'd done what he had,
When she lay there stiff and still;
But a sudden awe of the angry law
Struck his soul with an icy chill.
So to finish the fun so well begun.
He resolved himself to kill.

Then he took the sheet off his wife's cold feet,
And he twisted it into a rope,
And he hanged himself from the pantry shelf—
'Twas an easy end, let's hope—
In the face of death, with his latest breath,
He solemnly cursed the Pope.

But the strangest turn to the whole concern
Is only just beginin'!—
He went to h---, but his wife got well,
And she's still alive and sinnin'—
For the razor blade was German made,
But the sheet was—Irish Linen!

A Pint of Plain is Your Only Man

Flann O'Brien

In praise of Ireland's other source of comfort, dreams and satisfaction, its currency is rather more limited than that of the lays of uisce-beatha.

When things go wrong and will not come right,
Though you do the best you can,
When life looks black as the hour of night—
A PINT OF PLAIN IS YOUR ONLY MAN.

When money's tight and is hard to get
And your horse has also ran,
When all you have is a heap of debt—
A PINT OF PLAIN IS YOUR ONLY MAN.

When health is bad and your heart feels strange,
And your face is pale and wan,
When doctors say that you need a change,
A PINT OF PLAIN IS YOUR ONLY MAN.

When food is scarce and your larder bare
And no rashers grease your pan,
When hunger grows as your meals are rare—
A PINT OF PLAIN IS YOUR ONLY MAN.

In time of trouble and lousy strife,
You have still got a darlint plan,
You still can turn to a brighter life—
A PINT OF PLAIN IS YOUR ONLY MAN.

Ballad to a Traditional Refrain

Maurice James Craig

A pasquinade as lovingly deprecatory and as true now as when it was written more than thirty years ago.

Red brick in the suburbs, white horse on the wall,
Eyetalian marbles in the City Hall:
O stranger from England, why stand so aghast?
May the Lord in His mercy be kind to Belfast.

This jewel that houses our hopes and our fears
Was knocked up from the swamp in the last hundred years
But the last shall be first and the first shall be last:
May the Lord in His mercy be kind to Belfast.

We swore by King William there'd never be seen
An All-Irish Parliament at College Green,
So at Stormont we're nailing the flag to the mast:
May the Lord in His mercy be kind to Belfast.

O the bricks they will bleed and the rain it will weep,
And the damp Lagan fog lull the city to sleep;
It's to hell with the future and live on the past:
May the Lord in His mercy be kind to Belfast.

Thompson in Tir-na-n-Og

Gerald MacNamara

The play that with *The Drone* remains the most famous product of the Ulster Literary Theatre which was begun in friendly opposition to what was not yet quite the Abbey Theatre in 1902. The founders were Bulmer Hobson and David Parkhill and after a visit to the great guru they decided to strike out for themselves: "Damn Yeats, we'll write our own plays." MacNamara was the pen-name of Harry C. Morrow, one of a well-known family of painters and decorators (George, his brother, used to draw for *Punch*). The play was written as a three-acter for the Gaelic League but they rejected it because of the fun it poked at the heroes of Irish mythology. Morrow remoulded it as a one-act play. It was presented in the Ulster Hall on 9 December 1912 and has been popular ever since.

DRAMATIS PERSONAE.

HIGH KING OF TIR-NA-N-OG.

FINN.

ANGUS.

CUCHULAIN OF THE FORD.

CONAN MACMORNA.

MAEV.

GRANIA.

THOMPSON OF SCARVA.

Scene: The private grounds of the High King of Tir-na-n-Og.

King (seated C.) What has befallen our land this day, this land of eternal youth and happiness—beloved Tir-na-n-og. O sad is my heart, and my tongue is troubled with speaking in this new and curious language. Can it be that the knowledge of the Gaelic has utterly forsaken me, or is it but an evil spell which soon may pass away.

(Enter Finn.)

Finn (making a low bow.) Greetings to thee, O King of Tir-na-n-og.

King (bowing.) *(Aside.)* Poor Finn, he's got it too.

Finn. O King, I am in dire distress; I have been stricken with a malady which troubles me to understand. I have lost all words of Gaelic and in their stead I speak this language which must sound curious to thine ears.

(King shakes his head.)

Ah! I see 'tis useless to address the King in such a barbarous language. *(Turns to go off L.)*

King. Stay, noble Finn!

Finn. The gods be praised, you also speak this language.

King. In truth I do, but much against my will. What can be its portent?

Finn. Methinks it is an evil spell.

King. The thought occurred to me just now but I swiftly put it from me.

Finn. For what reason, O my King?

King. O fickle Finn, hast thou so soon forgotten? Remember we are still in Tir-na-n-og, which thou and I and others here have won by faithfulness and valour in the ancient land of Erin.

Finn. Yet spell it must be, for the feeling in my bones reminds me of the spells which Angus of the Danann people was wont to put upon us.

King. I do remember well those spells, yet Angus lodges in our peaceful land to-day, and none can say that he has practised these black arts of late.

Finn. 'Tis troth, but thou cans't never tell.

(Enter Angus L.)

Angus (bowing.)   Greetings to the High King of Tir-na-n-og, and to thee, O Finn, Ardrie of Benmadigan and ruler of the lands around Ardglass.

King.   You also speak in this strange tongue. Where hast thy Gaelic gone?

Angus.   O King, for reasons I was forced to exercise my power of casting spells.

Finn.   I told you so.

King.   I hope you have good reason, for my throat likes not this irritating language.

Angus.   I have good reason as you will shortly know.

Finn.   But what language is it that you've put upon us?

Angus.   I ordered purest English.

King.   English! What people are the English?

Angus.   They hail from the land beyond the Eastern Sea.

King.   What! Those barbarians! A people who were wont to paint their bodies red and white and blue.

Finn.   And who, we're told, did eat their near relations.

Angus.   From what I hear, they're much improved of late.

King.   But this is all beside the case—why put this English on us? We like it not; we much prefer our Gaelic.

Angus.   I own the feeling is most natural, but still I would have you understand that English now is spoken throughout our natal land.

King.   When did these tidings reach you?

Angus.   This morn at sunrise I did meet a strange young man from Erinn.

King.
Finn.   } From Erinn?

King.   And his name?

Angus.   His name is Thompson.

(Thunder and lightning.)

King.   Angus, what meaneth this?

Angus. I know not save that it be the mention of the name of "Thompson."

King. I've never known such name in Erinn.

Finn. Most like he is a son of Thomp.

King. I have no doubt, but who the—who is Thomp?

Angus. I know not, saving that he hails from Erinn.

King. How comes he here in Tir-na-n-og, where none has come for many thousand moons?

Angus. 'Tis very strange, but let me tell my story.

King. Proceed and make it brief.

Angus. This morning as I fed my birds of knowledge in my garden I espied a stranger. His garments were most strange, and his features were much stranger. I approached him and addressed him thus.

King. In English?

Angus. No, in Gaelic, for I knew no other tongue just then. I said "Ceud mile failte." At this he was most pleased but answered me in English.

King. And did you understand?

Angus. I did not, for to me it sounded like the bark of dogs. I was sore distressed, for I was anxious to have converse with him. I then recalled to mind my powers in ancient days of casting spells, so I tried to throw the Gaelic tongue upon him.

King. And did your spell not give entire satisfaction?

Angus. An utter failure.

Finn. 'Tis strange, for your great spells were never known to fail.

Angus. It was not that he *could not* speak the Gaelic. 'Twas that he *would not.*

King. And does he say he is of Irish birth?

Angus. He voweth so. He says he comes from Scarva.

King. Tell us more of this strange man from Scarva.

Angus. As I could not make him speak in Gaelic, I threw a spell upon myself and spoke to him in English.

King. How comes it that you cast a spell on us as well?

Angus.   And this, O King, is how it is—when first I spoke in English, I explained the nature of our country. How it was the land of youth and peace, and how I wished to bring him to our King and give him royal welcome.

King (impatiently.)   Bring Thompson forth, why keep him lingering at our royal gates? I long to see him.

Angus.   Alas it cannot be.

King.   For why?

Angus.   Because he ran away.

King.
Finn.   } He ran away!

Angus.   Yes, fleet as forest deer, and as he ran he shouted loud, "Too safe, it's an asylum."

King.   His conduct is most strange.

Angus.   And this is how it was. I put an English spell on everyone in Tir-na-n-og, that all might speak with him and make him feel "at home."

King.   Angus, thou hast always been most famous for thy wisdom. Come let us go in search of Thompson.

(*Enter Cuchulain and Conan.*)

Conan (excitedly.)   O High King of Tir-na-n-og, thy people are in deep distress, for they have lost their Gaelic.

King.   Fear not, O Conan, all will soon be well, and thou Cuchulain, do not tremble, for thy Gaelic words will soon come back again.

Cuchulain.   I tremble not, O king; I have no fear, nor ever had I.

King (patting him on the back.)   I know I know.

Cuchulain.   'Twas not much Gaelic that *I* ever spoke; my sword spoke for me.

King.   Well said Cuchulain, thy words are like a saga.

Conan (trembling.)   But why this strange departure from our ancient usage?

King.   'Twas Angus here who gave us power to speak like this.

Conan. But we dislike it.

King. Yes, yes, I know, but this was done that all might speak with Thompson who is a stranger.

Cuchulain. A stranger! This is something new in Tir-na-n-og.

King. Come, let us not delay. (*To Cuchulain and Conan.*) We go in search of Thompson.

(*Exit King, Finn, and Angus L.*)

Conan. This Thompson man must surely be a warrior brave from Erinn.

Cuchulain. What makes you say so, Conan?

Conan. No man comes here to Tir-na-n-og who has not done great deeds in battle.

Cuchulain. How comes it that you are here, O Conan?

Conan. Have I not done great deeds?

Cuchulain. Thy greatest was with Liagan.

Conan. Did I not cut his head clean off?

Cuchulain. No doubt, but still it was a foul.

Conan. All's fair in War.

Cuchulain. But that was most unfair. I'm told when Liagan's sword was o'er your head, in fear you called out (*mockingly*) "Truly thou art in more peril from the man behind than from the man in front." Liagan looked round and instantly you swept his head clean off and ran away.

Conan (*carelessly*). 'Twas but a jest.

Cuchulain. Such sorry jests do not become a follower of Finn.

Conan. What know you of Finn? You who belong to another cycle.

Cuchulain. Have I not heard from Finn's own lips, how he did strike with one great blow three princes' heads off?

Conan. *That* was a blow.

Cuchulain. You doubt his word! I'd rather have the word of Finn than coward's bonds like thine.

Conan. You call me coward, you who ran away from Ferdia at the Ford.

Cuchulain. I—I ran from Ferdia at the Ford? (*Threateningly.*) Say that once more and I will make two halves of you.

(*Enter Queen Maev and Grania.*)

O Maev, Queen of Connacht, fairest of all women, bear me witness, did I not hold the Ford 'gainst Ferdia?

Queen. O that thou surely didst, to my great sorrow, but who should say thee nay?

Cuchulain (*pointing at Conan*). 'Twas he, the coward.

Queen. Durst doubt the word of warriors of our cycle, thou low-born third cyclarian.

Grania (*to Queen*). Put no reproach upon my people. Our cycle is as good as thine. Our records of great deeds are not as numerous as thine, but *ours* at least are *true*.

Queen. How durst thou so address a Queen in whose veins flow the blood of gods. How durst thou, hussy!

(*Enter King, Angus and Finn R.*)

King. My children! my children! remember this is Tir-na-n-og where all is peace and love and joy.

Queen. I crave thy pardon, noble King, for being thus excited.

Grania. Our good tempers must have left us with our lovely Gaelic tongue.

(*King pats Grania on the back.*)

Cuchulain. Hast thou seen aught, O King, of Thompson?

King. The gods have smiled not on our efforts; our search was vain. (*Great cheering and laughing outside.*)

(*Enter Thompson L.—excited.*)

Thompson (*looking off.*) Away out o' that you unmannerly young rapscallions. (*To Cuchulain.*) Who the devil is them?

Cuchulain (*looking off.*) They are the children of Lir. They give you welcome to the land of youth.

Thompson. They have a quare way of doing it.

King. Did they say aught to give offence?

Thompson. They were shoutin' "Look at the ould lad."

King. I'm sure 'twas not intended for offence.

(*Thompson attempts to exit L.*)

Stay, O Thompson, stay a little longer.

(*Thompson stops in centre of stage beside King.*)

We give you welcome to our land this day. (*All bow.*) I have no doubt you have heard of all of us in story.

(*Thompson nods his head stupidly.*)

And you must also know what land you stand in.

Thompson. Well now, mister, I couldn't just name the district, but it must be either Co. Down or Armagh.

King. 'Tis neither one nor other—it's Tir-na-n-og.

Thompson. Which?

King. It's Tir-na-n-og, and I'm its King.

Thompson. Just what I suspected, an asylum.

King. We are all most anxious to discover how you left your native land.

Thompson. Well, the last thing I mind was yesterday about twelve o'clock. I was going to the fight at Scarva.

King. The fight! You died in battle! It is enough. Thou hast earned the just reward due to all warriors of Erinn. Although many moons have passed since last we had one worthy to approach our land, we hail thee more on that account. (*All bow to Thompson.*) But let me haste to introduce you to my people. This is Queen Maev, of whom no doubt you've often heard.

Thompson (*to King.*)   O aye, many's the time. How long is she in?

King.   We do not go by time in Tir-na-n-og.

Thompson (*jokingly.*)   All piece-work. Good evening, your Majesty, I needn't ask ye how ye are, for you're lookin' brave.

Queen.   Brave I am, and brave I ever was in the land of Erinn. There was not in Banba, nor yet in all Eire, a woman more excellent than myself. I was the most famous, the most powerful, and the best born.

Thompson (*cheerfully.*)   One of the best,

Queen (*proudly.*)   Not *one* of the best, but *the* best.

Thompson.   Aye, we'll let it go at that.

Queen.   Not even the half red Maev of Leinster was to be named beside me.

Thompson.   Not at all, she wasn't in the same street. (*Aside.*)   The weemin' are always the worst in these places.

King.   And this is Conan.

Thompson.   How are ye, Mister? (*Attempts to shake hands.*)

Conan (*grandly.*)   I am of the MacMornas.

Thompson.   Is that a fact? I didn't know them—Scotch, I suppose?

Conan.   Scots they were, but left their lands and sailed for Alba.

Thompson.   Just like the Scotch. Took single tickets, eh?

King.   And here is Grania, whose praises must be sung in Erinn even now.

Thompson.   That's a fact. I'm glad to meet you, Miss. (*Grania bows.*) (*Aside.*)   I don't think she's a luney.

King.   And this is Angus.

Angus.   My name must be familiar.

Thompson.   O aye, I've heard the name.

Angus.   I am of the race of the Danaan or people of the goddess Dana.

Thompson (*aside.*)   This is a bad case.

Angus. They were a people who delighted in beauty and gaiety and fond of fine apparel.

Thompson. So you're one of the "knuts."

Angus. My people were skilled in magic arts, and their harpers could make music that a man who heard it would forget all earthly things.

Thompson. But you couldn't fit your Gaelic unto me, ye ould messmerist. (*Angus scowls.*)

King. And this is Finn the Great.

Thompson (smiling.) Any friend of Finn McCool?

Finn. I *am* Finn MacCumhal.

Thompson (aside.) The sooner I get out of this place the better. (*Is going off L. when Cuchulain keeps him back.*)

Cuchulain. If thou art a fighting man from Erinn, thou must have heard of my great deeds.

Thompson. What's your name, Mister?

Cuchulain. Cuchulain.

Thompson. Koo-who?

Cuchulain. Cuchulain.

Thompson. Aye, it's a fine day.

Cuchulain. All days are fine in Tir-na-n-og.

Thompson. Is that a fact? Man *we* had a terrible wet summer this year.

Cuchulain. But hast thou never heard of me in Erinn?

Thompson. I'll tell you no lies, mister, I never did. What are ye, or what *were ye*?

Cuchulain. I was of the Red Branch, foremost of the fighting men of Ulster.

Thompson. Ulster! Put it there. (*Shakes hands.*) Why didn't ye tell me that before? (*Brings him down stage to front and whispers.*) Man, I took you for a luney like the rest. (*Points over his shoulder with his thumb.*)

Cuchulain. Were you ever in Ulster?

Thompson. Was I ever in Ulster—was I ever in—was I ever out of it?

Cuchulain. I hope that Ulster still holds sway in Erinn.

Thompson. I dunno about holdin' sway, but she can hold her own—and more.

Cuchulain. I am well pleased to hear it, for I did love and still do love my Ulster. What part of Ulster have you come from?

Thompson. Scarva.

Cuchulain. Lies Scarva east or west?

Thompson. It's on the Great Northern.

Cuchulain (reflectively.) Once I was the Great Northern.

Thompson (looks at Cuchulain pityingly and says aside.) He's as bad as the rest, poor sowl.

Cuchulain. O, how I fought for Ulster. *(Excitedly.)* When the great battle fury was on me.

Thompson. Now don't get excited, mister—I know what the battle fury is—I've had it often—every Twelfth—and Thirteenth.

Cuchulain. Whole hosts lay dead and bleeding at my feet.

Thompson. Now if you keep on talkin' like that they'll never let ye out.

Cuchulain. My skill in archery was never equalled.

Thompson. Now keep quiet and we'll get ye a minneture rifle.

Cuchulain. Alone I have routed an army.

Thompson (patronizingly patting Cuchulain on the shoulder.) Good man! good man!

Cuchulain. As I swept into battle with my gold bronze chariot, whole nations have trembled to hear the Ulster war cry on my lips.

Thompson (very excited, slapping Cuchulain on the back.) True blue! Ulster will fight and Ulster will be right. *(Assuming a military tone of voice.)* Form fours! Left turn! Quick march! (Exit L.) (The others on the stage look after Thompson and form in a cluster round the King.)

King. My people, I have grave doubts if this fair stranger is a worthy person for our Tir-na-n-og. He may have died in battle, but his manners please me not.

Conan.   He could never have passed the test of our Fiana.

Cuchulain.   The Red Branch would have scorned him.

Queen.   He comes not of a fighting brood.

Grania.   He may have been a kern, but not a chieftain.

King.   I think we're all agreed that Thompson's not a fit companion for our people here in Tir-na-n-og—but how are we to prove it?

Angus.   I have a plan, High King, if you would give your royal sanction.

King.   Speak on, wise Angus.

Angus.   I think a woman's wit would win us through this tribulation.

King.   What woman would you say?

Angus.   I think that Grania here could wheedle out this man's confession.

King (turning to Grania.)   Are you prepared to undertake this task?

Grania.   In truth there's nothing I'd like better.

(*Thompson is heard whistling "The Boyne Water." All on stage listen.*)

Conan.   'Tis Thompson, I can see him.

King.   Let us away. (*To Grania.*)   When you have discovered Thompson's history, give us a signal and we'll all return.

Grania.   What signal should I give?

King.   If you consider him a proper person, give three barks of a dog, but if you find that he's unworthy—

Grania.   I shall give three mews of a cat.

King.   S——s——h. (*Enter Thompson, very happy.*)   We leave you for a spell, O Thompson, till we make preparation for a royal feast in honour of your coming. Come, good people. (*All leave slowly R.*)   (*Grania giving the gladeye to Thompson.*)

Thompson.   I wish *you* wouldn't go, Grania, for you're all right anyway.

Grania (pouting.) Why did you leave us with so little ceremony?

Thompson. Ach, I was very dry.

Grania. And is your thirst quite satisfied?

Thompson. Not quite, I only had a pint—of mead, but as the barmaid would not take the money, I couldn't out of decency ask for more.

Grania (about to leave.) Everything is free in Tir-na-n-og.

Thompson. Ach, Grania, don't be leavin' me.

Grania. I wish to leave, yet some strange fascination holds me here.

Thompson. That's quare.

Grania (looking at Thompson sadly.) Last night I had a dream. I dreamt I saw a hero.

Thompson. A hero?

Grania. He stood like a flame against the flameless sky, and the whole sapphire of the heavens seemed to live in his fearless eyes.

Thompson. Well, well, did you know his face?

Grania. Not then, sweet Thompson.

Thompson (getting closer to Grania.) Have you saw him since?

Grania (getting quite close to Thompson.) I have to-day. He dwells in Tir-na-n-og.

Thompson (slipping his arm round Grania's waist.) Do I know him dear? Will you give me three guesses?

Grania. Cannot you guess in one? 'Twas none but you, O dearest Thompson. (*Leans her head on his chest.*)

Thompson. Call me Andy.

Grania. O Andy, Andy, my heart's desire. (*They both sit on tree trunk.*) Tell me dearest how you left old Erinn. You said that you were killed in battle.

Thompson. I was blew up.

Grania. "Blew up." How strange—what can be its portent?

Thompson.   Beg pardon.

Grania.   What does "blew up" mean?

Thompson.   A gun burst in my hand.

Grania.   A gun! What is a gun?

Thompson (aside.)   She's as bad as the rest. (*To Grania.*) A gun—well, a gun's a gun that shoots bullets that kills people.

Grania.   Ah, that must be a new thing.

Thompson.   Sowl, this wasn't a new thing.

Grania.   Where was this battle fought?

Thompson.   In Scarva. We have one every 13th July. Ach, it's a great sight. They come from all arts and parts to see the show. Excursion trains from Derry and Belfast. The papers used to make fun of us. Ach, but times is changed, for now the *News Letter* calls it a "pageant."

Grania.   And what part did you take in this great battle. Where you a Chieftain?

Thompson.   I was promoted this year to be one of King William's Generals.

Grania.   And you lead your fighting kerns into the heat of battle?

Thompson (confidently.)   Indeed, to tell you the truth, I never got the length of the field.

Grania.   That is strange.

Thompson.   I was takin' a short cut through the meadows, and while I was climbing a ditch, my ould gun burst in my hands, an' that is all I mind. I must a lay there all day and then maybe in the night I wandered about, not knowin' where I was, and then I must have fell asleep, and when I wakened up in the mornin' I didn't know where I was, and I'm damned if I know now—excuse me.

Grania.   And you know not if your army was victorious or not?

Thompson.   Sure I told you I was on King William's side. Of course we won the day.

Grania.   Why do you say "of course"? The fortunes of war are so uncertain.

Thompson. Sure it wasn't a real fight. It was a sham fight or a pageant fight.

Grania. A make believe. (*Thompson nods his head.*)

Thompson. Aye, the very thing.

Grania. But you *have* been in a *real* fight?

Thompson. O aye, I was in a scrap in Portadown last Sunday.

Grania. And whom were you fighting in Portadown?

Thompson. The Hibernians.

Grania (*shocked.*) The Hiberniana! But are not all the people in Erinn Hibernians?

Thompson. In sowl they're not.

Grania. Are all the people in Portadown Hiberniana?

Thompson. Talk sense woman dear.

Grania (*looking towards audience.*) Many changes must have come o'er Erinn since the days of Cuchulain and Oisin. Then we were all Hibernians. (*To Thompson.*) I wish dearest that you were an Hibernian too.

Thompson. You'll never see the day. (*Rising from the couch.*) And what's more, I'll have nothing more to do with you, for I'm no believer in mixed marriages.

Grania. Oh, Andy, tell me not that you fought *against* the Hibernians.

Thompson. In troth I did. (*Grania gives three mews of a cat.*) (*Aside.*) Ach, poor wee girl , she's the worst case of the lot. (*Moves towards L.*)

(*Enter all the others R.*)

King. Secure the prisoner!

(*Thompson is arrested by Cuchulain and Conan.*)

Thompson. Prisoner! What do you mean?

King. This land has always been reserved for warriors and patriots of Erinn. We consider you are neither one nor other, but by some mysterious hideous blunder you have been thrust upon us.

Thompson. If you let me alone I'll thrust myself out of this.

King. That is beyond your power. Our chief desire is to give you justice, and so we will now proceed with the trial. Finn read the charge.

Finn (unfolding parchment.) Andrew Thompson, late of Scarva, Ireland, you are charged with trespass in Tir-na-n-og, you having no right, title or authority to do the same, as you have never fought, died, or done anything in the cause of the Gael. What say you Andrew Thompson—Guilty or Not Guilty?

Thompson. Not guilty!

Finn. Are you, Andrew Thompson, prepared to stand your trial?

Thompson (trying to get away, but prevented by Cuchulain and Conan.) I wish you'd let me go home.

King. We will try you according to the ancient Brehon Laws.

Thompson. God help me now.

King. Who is the first witness?

Finn. Queen Maev, my lord.

King. Where did you see the prisoner first, my good woman?

Queen. On this very spot, my lord.

King. Is the prisoner at the bar in your opinion an Irishman?

Queen. He is not, my lord.

Thompson. You're a—it's a lie—my father and mother are Irish, and I am Irish too.

King. Why are you so convinced that this man is not Irish?

Queen. Because he speaks in a language foreign to Ireland.

King. And what language do you call it?

Queen. It is called English.

Thompson. But shure you are speaking English yourself.

Queen. But at present we are under a spell. (*Conan rises to his feet.*)

King. Hast thou anything to say, brave Conan?

Conan. I have, my lord. (*To Thompson.*) Can you speak Irish?

Thompson. I can not indeed, and I don't want to.

King. Answer the question, sir. We do not ask for your opinion.

Cuchulain. My lord, may I ask a few questions of the prisoner?

King. You may.

Cuchulain. Andrew Thompson, do you—?

Thompson. I object!

King. Answer the questions, sir.

Cuchulain. Do you still assert that you are Irish?

Thompson. Of coorse I do.

Cuchulain. And you admit that you do not speak the language of your country?

Thompson (*proudly.*) The language of my country is English.

Cuchulain. Answer me, sir. Can you speak Irish.

Thompson. I told you before that I couldn't, and I—

King. Keep silence!

Cuchulain. You affirm that you are Irish. Are you proud of that fact?

Thompson. Beg pardon?

Cuchulain (*in a loud voice.*) Are you proud of your country?

Thompson. I am, troth.

Cuchulain. But as you are speaking English, any man might call you "English."

Thompson. Wud he? Well, if he did, he wud never do it again.

Cuchulain. Why?

Thompson. Why? I'd break his jaw.

Angus. The remarks of this prisoner are most contradictory.

Thompson. Look here, mister, you howld yer tongue.

King. I cannot have such language in my court.

Thompson. But it's not fair. Here's three solicitors for the prosecution, an' not a sowl to speak for me.

Cuchulain. Now, sir, assuming that thou art an Irishman.

Thompson. Ach, don't bother me, ye ould quaker.

Cuchulain. You should at least have heard of the great deeds done by your ancestors in Ireland.

Thompson. And so I have.

Cuchulain. Let us hear something of the history of your country.

Thompson. Well, I know that King William won the Battle of the Boyne.

Cuchulain. When was this battle fought?

Thompson. On the 12th.

Cuchulain. Twelfth of what?

Thompson. Twelfth of July, Sixteen Hundred and Ninety.

Cuchulain. Were you present at this battle?

Thompson. Ach, you're all mad.

King. If this language continues I'll have you committed.

Cuchulain. If you had lived in this King's time would you have taken up arms against him?

Thompson. I would have fought for him tooth and nail.

Cuchulain. Was this William an Irishman?

Thompson. He was not.

Cuchulain (*looking round the Court.*) King William was not an Irishman. Now did this King, whom you seem to esteem so much, did he do any great deeds?

Thompson. Of coorse he did—he crossed the Boyne.

Cuchulain. He crossed the Boyne—how?

Thompson. On a horse—a white horse.

Cuchulain. Do you consider that a great deed?

Thompson. Of coorse I do; sure it's painted on all the Orangemen's banners.

Cuchulain. Who are these Orangemen?

Thompson. True-born sons of William (*proudly hitting his chest*), and I am one.

Cuchulain. Tell us something of your father—King William.

Thompson. Look here, mister, I don't like to hear you talkin' in that sarcastic way about King William.

Cuchulain. Tell us who he was.

Thompson. William the Third, Prince of Orange, of glorious, pious and immortal memory, come over from Holland.

Queen. He was a Dutch man.

Thompson. I suppose he must have been. I never thought of that before, but he bate King James anyway at the Battle of the Boyne.

Cuchulain. Who was this King James?

Thompson. You're very ignorant. He was King of England, and so was King William.

King. Both at the same time? It could not be.

Thompson. It's a fact—but the English people were sick of him.

King. Sick of whom?

Thompson. Of King James of coorse. Sure the English asked William to come over and reign in his place.

King. And he consented?

Thompson. Sartintly—and he chased James out of England and over the water to Ireland.

Cuchulain. And did the Irish people welcome this English King?

Thompson. Of coorse they did, for he was one of their own sort.

Cuchulain. Do you mean he was Irish after all?

Thompson. Not at all.

Cuchulain. Then what do you mean by "one of their own sort"?

Thompson. Look here, Mr. Cuckoo, I don't believe you're an Ulsterman at all.

Cuchulain. Do you mean to say that the Irish people had no desire for an Irish King?

Thompson (*looking L. and making an effort to get away, but kept back by Conan.*) Ach, I couldn't tell you. It all happened a long while ago.

Cuchulain.   Do your Orangemen rejoice in the victory of a foreign Prince over your own countrymen?

Thompson (in a tired voice.)   Aye.

Cuchulain.   And why?

Thompson (angry.)   Because we don't want Home Rule.

Cuchulain.   Are you too lazy to rule yourselves?

Thompson.   Ach, it's not that, for there's heaps of them in the South and West that want Home Rule.

Cuchulain.   What kind of people are these?

Thompson.   They're no class—a lot of Gaelic Leaguers and Hibernians.

Cuchulain.   Are you not a Hibernian?

Thompson.   If you insult me like that, I'll strike you.

Cuchulain (turning to the Court.)   On his own word the prisoner is no Irishman.

Thompson.   I didn't say that.

Angus.   But the word Hibernian is the Latin form of "Irishman."

Thompson.   I know nothin' about Latin, thank God.

Conan.   My lord, may I be permitted to ask a few questions?

King.   Yes, if they will lead to his conviction.

Conan (to Thompson.)   Have you ever heard of Bov the Red?

Thompson (hesitatingly.)   I don't think I mind hearing the name.

Conan.   Or the great deeds of the Fiana?

Thompson.   No, I don't think so.

Queen.   Have you heard of Ferdia's great fight with Cuchulain at the Ford?

Thompson (bored.)   I never did.

Angus.   Do you know anything of the story of the Dagda?

Thompson (shortly.)   No.

Grania.   Have you heard of the romance of Naisi and Deirdre?

Thompson.   I'll have nothing more to say to you, young woman.

King. Do you know aught of your country's history save that of this Battle of the Boyne?

Thompson. I know that King Charles was beheaded.

King. Was Charles an Irishman?

Thompson. No.

King. What more do you know?

Thompson. I know that King Henry VIII was a "Roman" till he was converted.

Cuchulain. Of course he wasn't an Irishman.

Thompson. He was not.

King. What has all this got to do with Ireland? We want to hear of Irish history.

Thompson. Shure they never teach you Irish history in the schools in Ireland.

Cuchulain. It is plain, my lord, that the prisoner has no knowledge even of the great deeds performed in Ireland. Now I would like to see if he has done any great deeds himself. (*To Thompson.*) Did you ever fight in the cause of the Gael?

Thompson. The which?

Cuchulain. Where you in the Red Branch?

Thompson. No, I was in the Black Preceptory.

Cuchulain. Were you a Chieftain?

Thompson. No, I was a bleacher.

Cuchulain. Did you ever fight against the enemies of your country?

Thompson. Many's the time.

Cuchulain. Who were these enemies?

Thompson. The peelers.

Finn. Who are these peelers?

Thompson. Fellows that lift you.

Finn. Strong men?

Thompson. There's no doubt they're a fine body of men and useful sometimes for putting down them terrible atrocities in the South and West.

Cuchulain. Then these peelers keep order in Ireland?

Thompson. They're supposed to.

King.   These peelers keep order in Ireland same as did the Fiana in our time, and you, sir, have come to Tir-na-n-og, you who have fought against the Fiana or peelers, as you now call them. It is but mockery to continue this trial any longer. I cannot condemn you to death, as such a thing as death is unknown in the land of youth, but I will put you to the test of fire. Have you anything to say?

Thompson.   These people are mad and dangerous, Your Most Gracious Majesty. If I am trespassing here it's not my fault, and you needn't blame me for knowing nothing about you and all these nice people, but anyway, sure I am doing you no harm.

King.   But you *are* doing us harm. You have bought with you into this land a disquieting influence; we can feel it in the air. During your short stay here you have already caused strife; even I cannot keep my temper in control.

Thompson.   But what am I doing on you? What's wrong with me?

King.   That is beyond my ken—perhaps it is your face—but sure we are that you and we cannot exist together in this peaceful land. You must stand or perish in the test. Take him away, and build a fire around the prisoner.

Thompson.   O, Your Most Excellent Majesty, Sir Edward—King Geo—ach, I don't know what I'm talking about. Will none of you have pity on me, or stretch out a hand to save me? I'm a widow man with a large family, and my life is not insured. Your Majesty, give me a chance.

King.   It is too late.

Thompson.   Ach, don't burn me, and I'll learn Gaelic, and I'll make the childer learn it—I will sowl, and I have a parrot at home that my uncle brought from foreign parts; it can only whistle "Dolly's Brae," but be heavens I'll learn it Gaelic too.

King.   Take him away, and apply the flame.

(*Thompson taken off, shouting "No surrender." Blaze off stage.*)

King. Tell me that Thompson has departed. See that he has not left his soul behind.

Finn. There's nothing left—not even his ashes.

(*Thunder.*)

King. Then why this anger in the elements?

Angus. I crave your pardon, O High King. It is the English spell that still is on us.

King. Make haste, remove it and let us have our Gaelic back again. (*Holding up goblet.*) SLANTE!

(CURTAIN.)

VIII
The Trimmin's on the Rosary

St Patrick's Breastplate

Anonymous

The "Lorica" or "Breastplate of St Patrick" has nothing to do
with the saint, but is a partly Druidic poem from the eighth
century. This version was done into English from the Whitley
Stokes translation of the Old Irish original.

I bind unto myself today
The strong Name of the Trinity,
By invocation of the same,
The Three in One, and One in Three.

I bind this day to me for ever,
By power of faith, Christ's Incarnation;
His baptism in the Jordan river;
His death on Cross for my salvation;
His bursting from the spiced tomb;
His riding up the heavenly way;
His coming at the day of doom;
I bind unto myself today.

I bind unto myself today
The virtues of the starlit heaven,
The glorious sun's life-giving ray,
The whiteness of the moon at even,
The flashing of the lightning free,
The whirling wind's tempestuous shocks,
The stable earth, the deep salt sea
Around the old eternal rocks.

I bind unto myself today
The power of God to hold and lead,
His eye to watch, His might to stay,

His ear to hearken to my need,
The wisdom of my God to teach,
His hand to guide, His shield to ward,
The word of God to give me speech,
His heavenly host to be my guard.

Christ be with me, Christ within me,
Christ behind me, Christ before me,
Christ beside me, Christ to win me,
Christ to comfort and restore me,
Christ beneath me, Christ above me,
Christ in quiet, Christ in danger,
Christ in hearts of all that love me,
Christ in mouth of friend and stranger.

I bind unto myself the Name,
The strong Name of the Trinity;
By invocation of the same,
The Three in One, and One in Three,
Of whom all nature hath creation,
Eternal Father, Spirit, Word,
Praise to the Lord of my salvation:
Salvation is of Christ the Lord.

Pangur Bán

Anonymous

Translated by Robin Flower

A translation of a poem found scribbled on a ninth-century manuscript in Austria. It is justly famous.

I and Pangur Bán, my cat,
'Tis a like task we are at;
Hunting mice is his delight,
Hunting words I sit all night.

Better far than praise of men
'Tis to sit with book and pen;
Pangur bears me no ill will,
He too plies his simple skill.

'Tis a merry thing to see
At our tasks how glad are we,
When at home we sit and find
Entertainment to our mind.

Oftentimes a mouse will stray
In the hero Pangur's way;
Oftentimes my keen thought set
Takes a meaning in its net.

'Gainst the wall he set his eye
Full and fierce and sharp and sly;
'Gainst the wall of knowledge I
All my little wisdom try.

When a mouse darts from its den,
O how glad is Pangur then!
O what gladness do I prove
When I solve the doubts I love!

So in peace our tasks we ply,
Pangur Bán, my cat, and I;
In our arts we find our bliss,
I have mine and he has his.

Practice every day has made
Pangur perfect in his trade;
I get wisdom day and night
Turning darkness into light.

Columcille the Scribe

Anonymous

Translated by Kuno Meyer

Certainly not by the Donegal saint but part of an eleventh-century cult revival. The sentiments expressed are very much in keeping with his life and mission.

My hand is weary with writing,
My sharp quill is not steady.
My slender beaked pen pours forth
A black draught of shining dark-blue ink.

A stream of the wisdom of blessed God
Springs from my fair brown shapely hand:
On the page it squirts its draught
Of ink of the green skinned holly.

My little dripping pen travels
Across the plain of shining books,
Without ceasing for the wealth of the great—
Whence my hand is weary with writing.

While Shepherds Watched Their Flocks by Night

Nahum Tate

Standard Christmas carol written by the seventeenth-century Poet Laureate and dramatist, one of the "improvers" of Shakespeare.

While shepherds watched their flocks by night,
    All seated on the ground,
The angel of the Lord came down,
    And glory shone around.

"Fear not," said he, for mighty dread
    Had seized their troubled mind;
"Glad tidings of great joy I bring
    To you and all mankind.

"To you, in David's town, this day
    Is born of David's line,
The Saviour, who is Christ the Lord,
    And this shall be the sign:

"The heavenly babe you there shall find
    To human view displayed,
All meanly wrapped in swaddling bands,
    And in a manger laid."

Thus spake the seraph; and forthwith
    Appeared a shining throng
Of angels, praising God, who thus
    Addressed their joyful song:

"All glory be to God on high,
   And to the earth be peace;
Good will henceforth from Heaven to men
   Begin and never cease."

Silent O Moyle

Thomas Moore

Song of Fionnuala, the daughter of Lir, whose nine hundred
years of swansdown exile culminated, in some versions of the
story, in baptism and death.

Silent O Moyle! be the roar of thy water,
Break not, ye breezes, your chain of repose,
While murmuring mournfully, Lir's lonely daughter
Tells to the night-star her tale of woes.
When shall the swan, her death-note singing,
Sleep, with wings in darkness furl'd?
When will heaven, its sweet bell ringing,
Call my spirit from this stormy world?

Sadly, O Moyle! to thy winter wave weeping.
Fate bids me languish long ages away!
Yet still in her darkness doth Erin lie sleeping,
Still doth the pure light its dawning delay!
When will that day-star, mildly springing,
Warm our isle with peace and love?
When will heaven, its sweet bell ringing,
Call my spirit to the fields above?

All Things Bright and Beautiful

Cecil Frances Alexander

One of three hymns originally written for children by Cecil Frances Humphreys when she ran a Sunday School in Strabane and upon which her world-wide fame rests. This was before she married the Rev. William Alexander, who became Bishop of Derry and, after her death, Archbishop of Armagh. A series of stained glass windows in the baptistry of St Columb's Cathedral in Derry celebrates these hymns, the present one, "There is a Green Hill Far Away" and "Once in Royal David's City".

All things bright and beautiful,
 All creatures great and small,
All things wise and wonderful,
 The Lord God made them all.

Each little flower that opens,
 Each little bird that sings,
He made their glowing colours,
 He made their tiny wings.

The rich man in his castle,
 The poor man at his gate,
God made them, high or lowly,
 And ordered their estate.

The purple-headed mountain,
 The river running by,
The sunset and the morning
 That brightens up the sky—

The cold wind in the winter,
    The pleasant summer sun,
The ripe fruits in the garden—
    He made them every one;

The tall trees in the greenwood,
    The meadows where we play,
The rushes by the water
    We gather every day—

He gave us eyes to see them,
    And lips that we might tell
How great is God Almighty,
    Who has made all things well.

"We are the music-makers"

Arthur O'Shaughnessy

Part of *Ode,* the one poem of a one-poem poet, and often quoted by those who believe that poetry is misty, romantic and crepuscular.

We are the music-makers,
   And we are the dreamers of dreams,
Wandering by lone sea-breakers,
   And sitting by desolate streams;—
World-losers and world-forsakers.
   On whom the pale moon gleams:
Yet we are the movers and shakers
   Of the world for ever, it seems.

We, in the ages lying
   In the buried past of the earth,
Built Nineveh with our sighing,
   And Babel itself with our mirth;
And o'erthrew them with prophesying
   To the old of the new world's worth;
For each age is a dream that is dying,
   Or one that is coming to birth.

Sheep and Lambs

Katherine Tynan

The great choir piece by Yeats's Catholic friend from Clondalkin.

All in the April evening,
   April airs were abroad,
The sheep with their little lambs
   Passed me by on the road.

The sheep with their little lambs
   Passed me by on the road;
All in the April evening
   I thought on the Lamb of God.

The lambs were weary, and crying
   With a weak, human cry.
I thought on the Lamb of God
   Going meekly to die.

Up in the blue, blue mountains
   Dewy pastures are sweet;
Rest for the little bodies,
   Rest for the little feet,

But for the Lamb of God,
   Up on the hilltop green,
Only a cross of shame
   Two stark crosses between.

All in the April evening,
   April airs were abroad;
I saw the sheep with their lambs,
   And thought on the Lamb of God.

The Trimmin's on the Rosary

John A. O'Brien

A long but once very popular poem by an Australian priest
recalling the great prayer-feast that inevitably followed the
family Rosary which gave such succour to mothers and caused
much impatience in the younger members of the family.

Ah, the memories that find me now my hair is turning
        gray,
Drifting in like painted butterflies from paddocks far away;
Dripping dainty wings in fancy—and the pictures, fading
        fast,
Stand again in rose and purple in the album of the past.
There's the old slab dwelling dreaming by the wistful,
        watchful trees,
Where the coolabahs are listening to the stories of the
        breeze;
There's a homely welcome beaming from its big, bright
        friendly eyes,
With The Sugarloaf behind it blackened in against the skies;
There's the same dear happy circle round the boree's cheery
        blaze
With a little Irish mother telling tales of other days.
She had one sweet, holy custom which I never can forget,
And a gentle benediction crowns her memory for it yet;
I can see that little mother still and hear her as she pleads,
"Now it's getting on to bed-time; all you childer get your
        beads."
There were no steel-bound conventions in that old slab
        dwelling free;
Only this—each night she lined us up to say the Rosary;
E'en the stranger there, who stayed the night upon his
        journey, knew
He must join the little circle, ay, and take his decade too.

I believe she darkly plotted, when a sinner hove in sight
Who was known to say no prayer at all, to make him stay
　　　the night.
Then we'd softly gather round her, and we'd speak in
　　　accents low,
And pray like Sainted Dominic so many years ago;
And the little Irish mother's face was radiant, for she knew
That "where two or three are gathered" He is gathered
　　　with them too.
O'er the paters and the aves how her reverent head would
　　　bend!
How she'd kiss the cross devoutly when she counted to the
　　　end!
And the visitor would rise at once, and brush his
　　　knees—and then
He'd look very, very foolish as he took the boards again.
She had other prayers to keep him. They were long, long
　　　prayers in truth;
And we used to call them "Trimmin's" in my disrespectful
　　　youth.
She would pray for kith and kin, and all the friends she'd
　　　ever known,
Yes, and everyone of us could boast a "trimmin" all his
　　　own.
She would pray for all our little needs, and every shade of
　　　care
That might darken o'er The Sugarloaf, she'd meet it with a
　　　prayer.
She would pray for this one's "sore complaint," or that
　　　one's "hurted hand,"
Or that someone else might make a deal and get "that bit of
　　　land";
Or that Dad might sell the cattle well, and seasons good
　　　might rule,
So that little John, the weakly one, might go away to
　　　school.
There were trimmin's, too, that came and went; but ne'er
　　　she closed without
Adding one for something special "none of you must speak
　　　about."

Gentle was that little mother, and her wit would sparkle
free,
But she'd murder him who looked around while at the
Rosary:
And if perchance you lost your beads, disaster waited you,
For the only one she'd pardon was "himself"—because she
knew
He was hopeless, and 'twas sinful what excuses he'd invent,
So she let him have his fingers, and he cracked them as he
went,
And, bedad, he wasn't certain if he'd counted five or ten,
Yet he'd face the crisis bravely, and would start around
again;
But she tallied all the decades, and she'd block him on the
spot,
With a "Glory, Daddah, Glory!" and he'd "Glory" like a
shot.
She would portion out the decades to the company at large;
But when she reached the trimmin's she would put herself
in charge;
And it oft was cause for wonder how she never once
forgot,
But could keep them in their order till she went right
through the lot.
For that little Irish mother's prayers embraced the country
wide;
If a neighbour met with trouble, or was taken ill, or died,
We could count upon a trimmin'—till, in fact, it got that
way
That the Rosary was but trimmin's to the trimmin's we
would say.
Then "himself" would start keownrawing—for the public
good, we thought—
"Sure you'll have us here till mornin'. Yerra, cut them
trimmin's short!"
But she'd take him very gently, till he softened by
degrees—
"Well, then, let us get it over. Come now, all hands to their
knees."

So the little Irish mother kept her trimmin's to the last,
Ever growing as the shadows o'er the old selection passed;
And she lit our drab existence with her simple faith and
　　　love,
And I know the angels lingered near to bear her prayers
　　　above,
For her children trod the path she trod, nor did they later
　　　spurn
To impress her wholesome maxims on their children in
　　　their turn.
Ay, and every "sore complaint" came right, and every
　　　"hurted hand";
And we made a deal from time to time, and got "that bit of
　　　land";
And Dad did sell the cattle well; and little John, her pride,
Was he who said the Mass in black the morning that she
　　　died;
So her gentle spirit triumphed—for 'twas this, without a
　　　doubt,
Was the very special trimmin' that she kept so dark about.

But the years have crowded past us, and the fledglings all
　　　have flown,
And the nest beneath The Sugarloaf no longer is their own;
For a hand has written "*finis*" and the book is closed for
　　　good—
There's a stately red-tiled mansion where the old slab
　　　dwelling stood;
There the stranger has her "evenings," and the formal
　　　supper's spread,
But I wonder has she "trimmin's" now, or is the Rosary
　　　said?
Ah, those little Irish mothers passing from us one by one!
Who will write the noble story of the good that they have
　　　done?
All their children may be scattered, and their fortunes
　　　windwards hurled,
But the Trimmin's on the Rosary will bless them round the
　　　world.

To My Daughter Betty, The Gift of God

Thomas Kettle

Sadly prophetic and most attractive sonnet by one of the wittiest and most literary of Irish men of affairs in the post-Parnell era. The last line is often quoted but no one is quite sure what exactly it meant to the author.

In wiser days, my darling rosebud, blown
To beauty proud as was your mother's prime,
In that desired, delayed, incredible time,
You'll ask why I abandoned you, my own,
And the dear heart that was your baby throne,
To dice with death. And, oh! they'll give you rhyme
And reason: some will call the thing sublime,
And some decry it in a knowing tone.
So here, while the mad guns curse overhead,
And tired men sigh, with mud for couch and floor,
Know that we fools, now with the foolish dead,
Died not for flag, nor King, nor Emperor,
But for a dream, born in a herdsman's shed,
And for the secret Scripture of the poor.

In the field, before Guillemont, Somme, September 4, 1916.

By the Short Cut to the Rosses

Nora Hopper

One of the songs that when it was sung by John McCormack
caused Rachmaninov to remark, "John, you sing a good song
well but you sing an inferior song *magnificently!*"

By the short cut to the Rosses,
   A fairy girl I met;
I was taken by her beauty
   Just like fishes in the net.
The fern uncurled to look at her
   So very fair was she,
With her hair as bright as seaweed
   That floats in from the sea.

By the short cut to the Rosses,
   'Twas on the first of May,
I heard the fairies piping,
   And they piped my heart away;
They piped 'till I was mad with joy,
   But when I was alone,
I found my heart was piped away—
   And in my breast, a stone.

By the short cut to the Rosses
   'Till I go never more,
Lest she should also steal my soul,
   Who stole my heart before.
Lest she should take my soul and crush it,
   Like a dead leaf in her hand,
For the short cut to the Rosses
   Is the way to fairyland.

IX

Sweet Inishfallen, Fare Thee Well

The Moon Behind the Hill

William Kenneally

A song printed in *The Nation* by the future mayor of Kilkenny
which had the distinction of becoming a regular feature of the
repertoire of the Christy Minstrels, a black-faced troupe who
made the work of Stephen Foster famous.

I watched last night the rising moon,
Upon a foreign strand,
Till mem'ries came like flowers of June,
Of home and fatherland:
I dreamt I was a child once more,
Beside the rippling rill,
When first I saw, in days of yore
The moon behind the hill.

It brought me back the visions grand
That purpled boyhood's dreams,
Its youthful loves, its happy land,
As bright as morning beams;
It brought me back my own sweet Nore.
The castle and the mill,
Until my eyes could see no more
The moon behind the hill.

It brought me back a mother's love,
Until, in accents wild,
I prayed her from her home above
To guard her lonely child;
It brought me one across the wave
To live in mem'ry still:
It brought me back my Kathleen's grave,
The moon behind the hill.

And there, beneath the silv'ry sky
I lived life o'er again;
I counted all its hopes gone by,
I wept at all its pain;
And when I'm gone, oh! may some tongue,
The minstrel's wish fulfil,
And still remember him who sang,
"The Moon behind the Hill."

The Irish Emigrant

Lady Dufferin

One of the great songs of exile written by the witty grand-
daughter of Sheridan and wife of the Marquis of Dufferin and
Ava.

I'm sitting on the stile, Mary,
   Where we sat side by side,
On a bright May morning, long ago,
   When first you were my bride.
The corn was springing fresh and green,
   And the lark sang loud and high,
And the red was on your lip, Mary,
   And the love-light in your eye.
The place is little changed, Mary,
   The day is bright as then,
The lark's loud song is in my ear,
   And the corn is green again;
But I miss the soft clasp of your hand,
   And the breath warm on my cheek,
And I still keep listening for the words
   You nevermore may speak,
You nevermore may speak.

'Tis but a step down yonder lane,
   The little church stands near—
The church were we were wed, Mary—
   I see the spire from here;
But the graveyard lies between, Mary,
   My step might break your rest,
Where you, my darling, lie asleep
   With your baby on your breast.

I'm very lonely now, Mary,
    The poor make no new friends;
But, oh, they love the better still
    The few our Father sends.
And you were all I had, Mary,
    My blessing and my pride;
There's nothing left to care for now
    Since my poor Mary died.

Yours was the good, brave heart, Mary,
    That still kept hoping on,
When trust in God had left my soul,
    And half my strength was gone.
There was comfort ever on your lip,
    And the kind look on your brow;
I bless you, Mary, for that same,
    Though you can't hear me now.

I'm bidding you a long farewell,
    My Mary, kind and true!
But I'll not forget you, darling,
    In the land I'm going to.
They say there's bread and work for all,
    And the sun shines always there;
But I'll not forget old Ireland
    Were it fifty times as fair.

O Bay of Dublin

Lady Dufferin

Another poem by the Scrabo marchioness and the first of
many to rhyme "Dublin" with "troublin".

O Bay of Dublin! my heart you're troublin'
Your beauty haunts me like a fevered dream,
Like frozen fountains that the sun sets bubblin',
My heart's blood warms when I but hear your name.
And never till this life pulse ceases,
My earliest thoughts you'll cease to be;
O there's no one here knows how fair that place is,
And no one cares how dear it is to me.

Sweet Wicklow mountains! the sunlight sleeping
On your green banks is a picture rare;
You crowd around me like young girls peeping,
And puzzling me to say which is most fair;
As though you'd see your own sweet faces,
Reflected in that smooth and silver sea,
O! my blessing on those lovely places,
Though no one cares how dear they are to me.

How often when at work I'm sitting,
And musing sadly on the days of yore,
I think I see my Katey knitting
And the children playing round the cabin door;
I think I see the neighbours' faces
All gathered round, their long-lost friend to see.
O! though no one knows how fair that place is,
Heaven   knows how dear my poor home was to me.

Song from the Backwoods

T. D. Sullivan

A song of early Fenian times, inspired by O'Leary's American visit.

Deep in Canadian woods we've met,
   From one bright island flown;
Great is the land we tread, but yet
   Our hearts are with our own.
And ere we leave this shanty small,
   While fades the autumn day,
     We'll toast old Ireland! dear old Ireland!
     Ireland, boys hurra!

We've heard her faults a hundred times,
   The new ones and the old,
In songs and sermons, rants and rhymes,
   Enlarged some fifty-fold.
But take them all, the great and small,
   And this we've got to say—
     Here's dear old Ireland! good old Ireland!
     Ireland, boys, hurra!

We know that brave and good men tried
   To snap her rusty chain,
That patriots suffered, martyrs died,
   And all, 'tis said, in vain;
But no, boys no! a glance will show
   How far they've won their way—
     Here's good old Ireland! loved old Ireland!
     Ireland, boys, hurra!

We've seen the wedding and the wake,
  The pattern and the fair;
The stuff they take, the fun they make,
  And the heads they break down there
With a loud "hurroo" and a "pillalu,"
  And a thundering "clear the way!"
    Here's gay old Ireland! dear old Ireland!
    Ireland, boys, hurra!

And well we know in the cool grey eyes,
  When the hard day's work is o'er.
How soft and sweet are the words that greet
  The friends who meet once more;
With "Mary machree!" and "My Pat! 'tis he!"
  And "My own heart night and day!"
    Ah, fond old Ireland! dear old Ireland!
    Ireland, boys, hurra!

And happy and bright are the groups that pass
  From their peaceful homes, for miles,
O'er fields, and roads, and hill, to Mass,
  When Sunday morning smiles!
And deep the zeal their true hearts feel
  When low they kneel and pray.
    Oh dear old Ireland! blest old Ireland!
    Ireland, boys, hurra!

But deep in Canadian woods we've met,
  And we never may see again
The dear old isle where our hearts are set,
  And our first fond hopes remain!
But come, fill up another cup,
  And with every sup let's say—
    Here's loved old Ireland! good old Ireland!
    Ireland, boys, hurra!

The Old Bog Road

Teresa Brayton

Another favourite tear-jerking song of exile written by one who had first-hand experience of home-sickness.

My feet are here on Broadway this blessed harvest morn,
But O the ache that's in them for the spot where I was
    born.
My weary hands are blistered from work in cold and heat,
And O to swing a scythe to-day, thro' fields of Irish wheat.
Had I the chance to wander back, or own a king's abode,
'Tis soon I'd see the hawthorn tree by the Old Bog Road.

When I was young and restless, my mind was ill at ease,
Through dreaming of America, and gold beyond the seas,
O sorrow take their money, 'tis hard to get that same,
And what's the world to any man, where no one speaks his
    name.
I've had my day and here I am, with building bricks for
    load,
A long three thousand miles away, from the Old Bog
    Road.

My mother died last spring tide, when Ireland's fields were
    green,
The neighbours said her waking was the finest ever seen.
There were snowdrops and primroses; piled up beside her
    bed,
And Ferns Church was crowded, when her funeral Mass
    was said.
But there was I on Broadway, with building bricks for
    load,
When they carried out her coffin, from the Old Bog Road.

There was a decent girl at home, who used to walk with
    me,
Her eyes were soft and sorrowful, like sunbeams on the
    sea,
Her name was Mary Dwyer; but that was long ago,
And the ways of God are wiser, than the things a man may
    know.
She died the year I left her, with building bricks for load,
I'd best forget the times we met, on the Old Bog Road.

Ah! life's a weary puzzle, past finding out by man,
I take the day for what it's worth and do the best I can.
Since no one cares a rush for me; what needs to make a
    moan,
I go my way, and draw my pay and smoke my pipe alone,
Each human heart must know its grief, tho' little be its
    load,
So God be with you Ireland, and the Old Bog Road.

Off to Philadelphia

Anonymous

A song dignified by a vigorous recording by McCormack.

My name is Paddy Leary,
From a spot called Tipperary.
The hearts of all the girls I'm a thorn in;
But before the break of morn,
Faith, 'tis they'll be all forlorn,
For I'm off to Philadelphia in the morning.

Chorus
With my bundle on my shoulder,
Faith, there's no man could be bolder,
I'm leaving dear old Ireland without warnin'.
For I lately took the notion
To cross the briny ocean,
For I start for Philadelphia in the mornin'.

There's a girl called Kate Malone,
Whom I'd hoped to call my own,
And to see my little cabin floor adornin';
But my heart is sad and weary,
How can she be Mrs. Leary,
If I start for Philadelphia in the mornin'?

Chorus

When they told me I must leave the place,
I tried to keep a cheerful face,
For to show my heart's deep sorrow I was scornin'
But the tears will surely blind me,
For the friends I leave behind me,
When I start for Philadelphia in the mornin'

Chorus

But tho' my bundle's on my shoulder,
And there's no man could be bolder,
Tho' I'm leavin' now the spot that I was born in;
Yet some day I'll take the notion
To come back across the ocean
To my home in dear old Ireland in the mornin'.

Come Back, Paddy Reilly

Percy French

One of three very touching songs of homeland written with great compassion by a master. His sojourn in County Cavan as Inspector of Drains gave him his inspiration for this piece. The innocent racialism of "the belles of the Blackamoor brand, And the chocolate shapes of Feegee" places it in a less sensitive age.

The Garden of Eden has vanished they say,
But I know the lie of it still.
Just turn to the left at the bridge of Finea,
And stop when half-way to Cootehill.
'Tis there I will find it, I know sure enough,
When fortune has come to my call.
Oh, the grass it is green around Ballyjamesduff,
And the blue sky is over it all!
And tones that are tender and tones that are gruff
Are whispering over the sea,
"Come back, Paddy Reilly, to Ballyjamesduff,
Come home, Paddy Reilly, to me."

My Mother once told me that when I was born,
The day that I first saw the light,
I looked down the street on that very first morn
And gave a great crow of delight.
Now most new-born babies appear in a huff
And start with a sorrowful squall,
But I knew I was born in Ballyjamesduff
And that's why I smiled on them all!
The baby's a man now, he's toil-worn and tough,
Still, whispers come over the sea,
"Come back, Paddy Reilly, to Ballyjamesduff,
Come home, Paddy Reilly, to me."

The night that we danced by the light o' the moon,
Wid Phil to the fore wid his flute,
When Phil threw his lip over "Come agin soon,"
He'd dance the foot out o' yer boot!
The day that I took long Magee by the scruff,
For slanderin' Rosie Kilrain;
Then marchin' him straight out of Ballyjamesduff,
Assisted him into a drain.
Oh! sweet are me dreams as the dudeen I puff,
Of whisperings over the sea:
"Come back, Paddy Reilly, to Ballyjamesduff,
Come home, Paddy Reilly, to me."

I've loved the young weeman of every land,
That always came easy to me;
Just barrin' the belles of the Blackamore brand,
And the chocolate shapes of Feegee.
But that sort of love is a moonshining stuff,
And never will addle me brain;
For bells will be ringin' in Ballyjamesduff
For me and me Rosie Kilrain.
And all through their glamour, their gas, and their guff,
A whisper comes over the sea:
"Come back, Paddy Reilly, to Ballyjamesduff,
Come home, Paddy Reilly to me."

The Mountains of Mourne

Percy French

French had not visited Newcastle when he wrote this song. He was staying in Rush, County Dublin, whence on a clear day he could see the Mourne Mountains stand out in sharp relief beyond the plains of Meath and the Cooley Hills. The music was written by one of his most empathetic colleagues, The Rev. Dr Houston Collisson .

Oh, Mary, this London's a wonderful sight,
Wid the people here workin' by day and by night:
   They don't sow potatoes, nor barley, nor wheat,
    But there's gangs o' them diggin' for gold in the street—
At least, when I axed them, that's what I was told,
So I just took a hand at this diggin' for gold,
   But for all that I found there, I might as well be
   Where the Mountains o' Mourne sweep down to the sea.

I believe that, when writin', a wish you expressed
As to how the fine ladies in London were dressed.
   Well, if you'll believe me, when axed to a ball,
   They don't wear a top to their dresses at all!
Oh, I've seen them meself, and you could not, in thrath,
Say if they were bound for a ball or a bath—
   Don't be startin' them fashions now, Mary Machree,
   Where the Mountains o' Mourne sweep down to the sea.

I seen England's King from the top of a 'bus—
I never knew him, though he means to know us:
   And though by the Saxon we once were oppressed,
   Still, I cheered—God forgive me—I cheered wid the rest.
And now that he's visited Erin's green shore,
We'll be much better friends than we've been heretofore,

When we've got all we want, we're as quiet as can be
Where the Mountains o' Mourne sweep down to the sea.

You remember young Peter O'Loughlin, of course—
Well, here he is now at the head o' the Force.
I met him to-day, I was crossin' the Strand,
And he stopped the whole street wid wan wave of his
hand:
And there we stood talking of days that are gone,
While the whole population of London looked on;
But for all these great powers, he's wishful like me,
To be back where dark Mourne sweeps down to the sea.

There's beautiful girls here—oh, never mind!
With beautiful shapes Nature never designed,
And lovely complexions, all roses and crame,
But O'Loughlin remarked wid regard to them same:
"That if at those roses you venture to sip,
The colour might all come away on your lip,"
So I'll wait for the wild rose that's waitin' for me—
Where the Mountains o' Mourne sweep down to the sea.

The Emigrant's Letter

Percy French

When French and Collisson were leaving for the States on a
concert tour they overheard one of the steerage passengers
say, "They're cutting the corn in Creeshla today". The result
was this very popular song and recitation.

Dear Danny,
I'm takin' the pen in me hand
To tell you we're just out o' sight o' the land;
　　In the grand Allan liner we're sailin' in style,
　　But we're sailin' away from the Emerald Isle;
And a long sort o' sigh seemed to rise from us all
As the waves hid the last bit of ould Donegal.
　　Och! it's well to be you that is takin' yer tay
　　Where they're cuttin' the corn in Creeshla the day.

I spoke to the captain—he won't turn her round,
And if I swum back I'd be apt to be drowned,
　　So here I must stay—oh! I've no cause to fret,
　　For their dinner was what you might call a banquet
But though it is "sumpchus," I'd swop the whole lot
For the ould wooden spoon and the stirabout pot;
　　And sweet Katey Farrell a-wettin' the tay
　　Where they're cuttin' the corn in Creeshla the day!

If Katey is courted by Patsey or Mick,
Put a word in for me with a lump of a stick,
　　Don't kill Patsey outright, he has no sort of a chance
　　But Mickey's a rogue you might murther at wance
For Katey might think as the longer she waits
A boy in the hand is worth two in the States:
　　And she'll promise to honour, to love and obey
　　Some robber that's roamin' round Creeshla the day.

Good-bye to you Dan, there's no more to be said,
And I think the salt wather's got into me head,
   For it dreeps from me eyes when I call to me mind,
   The friends and the colleen I'm leavin' behind;
Oh, Danny, she'll wait; whin I bid her good-bye,
There was just the laste taste of a tear in her eye,
   And a break in her voice whin she said "you might stay,
   But plaze God you'll come back to ould Creeshla some
      day."

Corrymeela

Moira O'Neill

Moira O'Neill came from the Glens and celebrated North Antrim and Rathlin in two volumes called *Songs of the Glens of Antrim.* "Corrymeela" is her best known poem.

Over here in England I'm helpin' wi' the hay,
    An' I wisht I was in Ireland the livelong day;
Weary on the English hay, an' sorra take the wheat!
    Och! Corrymeela an' the blue sky over it.

There's a deep dumb river flowin' out beyont the heavy
    trees,
The livin' air is moithered wi' the hummin' o' the bees;
I wisht I'd hear the Claddagh burn go runnin' through the
    heat
    Past Corrymeela, wi' the blue sky over it.

The people that's in England is richer nor the Jews,
    There not the smallest gossoon but thravels in his shoes!
I'd give the pipe between me teeth to see a barefut child.
    Och! Corrymeela an' the low south wind.

Here's hands so full o' money an' hearts so full o' care
    By the luck o' love I'd still go light for all I did go bare.
'God save ye, colleen dhas,' I said: the girl she thought me
    wild.
    Far Corrymeela, an' the low south wind.

D'ye mind me now, the song at night is mortial hard to
    raise,
    The girls are heavy goin' here, the boys are ill to please;

When one'st I'm out this workin' hive, 'tis I'll be back
  again—
  Ay, Corrymeela, in the same soft rain.

The puff o' smoke from one ould roof before an English
  town!
  For a shaugh wid Andy Feelan here I'd give a silver
    crown,
For a curl o' hair like Mollie's ye'll ask the like in vain,
  Sweet Corrymeela, an' the same soft rain.

Mary from Dungloe

Anonymous

Another plaintive song of exile recently revived and made the theme-song of the Mary from Dungloe festival held in July/August each year.

Oh, then, fare ye well sweet Donegal, the Rosses and
      Gweedore
I'm crossing the main ocean, where the foaming billows
      roar.
It breaks my heart from you to part, where I spent many
      happy days
Farewell to kind relations, for I'm bound for Amerikay.

Oh, my love is tall and handsome and her age is scarce
      eighteen
She far exceeds all other fair maids when she trips over the
      green
Her lovely neck and shoulders are fairer than the snow
Till the day I die I'll ne'er deny my Mary from Dungloe.

If I was at home in Sweet Dungloe a letter I would write
Kind thoughts would fill my bosom for Mary my delight
'Tis in her father's garden, the fairest violets grow
And 'twas there I came to court the maid, my Mary from
      Dungloe.

Ah then, Mary you're my heart's delight my pride and only
      care
It was your cruel father, would not let me stay there.
But absence makes the heart grow fond and when I'm o'er
      the main
May the Lord protect my darling girl till I return again.

And I wished I was in Sweet Dungloe and seated on the
    grass
And by my side a bottle of wine and on my knee a lass.
I'd call for liquor of the best and I'd pay before I would go
And I'd roll my Mary in my arms in the town of Sweet
    Dungloe.

Biographical Index

AE (see George Russell)

CECIL FRANCES ALEXANDER was born Humphreys in County Wicklow in 1818 but spent most of her adult life in the North. She married William Alexander in 1851, after her most famous hymns were already written. "Once in Royal David's City", "All Things Bright and Beautiful" and "There is a Green Hill Far Away" were included in *Hymns for Little Children* (1848) which she wrote for her Sunday School in Strabane. She died in 1895 in Derry, where her husband was bishop. He afterwards became Archbishop of Armagh. She was buried in Derry Cemetery and it is believed that hers was the first Protestant grave to have a cross as a memorial.

WILLIAM ALLINGHAM was born in Ballyshannon, County Donegal, in 1824 and served as a customs official at posts all over the North of Ireland. His poems were often sold as broadsheets and it pleased his shy soul to discover ballad-mongers trying to sell him copies of his own poems. He went to live in England and was a member of the Pre-Raphaelite brotherhood and a friend of Tennyson. He died in 1889 and was buried in Ballyshannon.

Sir JONAH BARRINGTON was born near Abbeyleix in 1760 and after graduation from Trinity was called to the bar in 1788. A man of wit and ability, he was strongly opposed to the Act of Union but with characteristic quixotry acted as agent for Pitt's bribers. His modern fame rests upon *Personal Sketches,* memoirs written in his late sixties. These are a funny and graphic account of the heyday of the Big House. He left Ireland to avoid proceedings for misappropriation of funds and died in Versailles in 1834.

TERESA BRAYTON was born Teresa Boylan at Kilbrook, near Cloncurry in County Kildare in 1868 and qualified as a teacher. She emigrated to the US when she was twenty and later wrote poems under the pseudonym T. B. Kilbrook. She married Richard Brayton. She made several visits home to Ireland before 1916 and became friendly with Pearse and the other 1916 leaders. She came home to Ireland to live in the twenties and died in Bray.

RAYMOND COLVILLE CALVERT was born in Helen's Bay, County Down, in 1906. He was educated at Queen's University and though his life was spent as a stockbroker he maintained his connection with the university. His claim to literary fame rests upon the mock-ballad (really an extended Ulster joke) "The Ballad of William Bloat" which was composed for a University Drama Society party. He died in 1959.

JOSEPH CAMPBELL (alias Seosamh Mac Cathmhaoil) was born in Belfast in 1879. He was part of the Ulster Literary Revival associated with the Ulster Literary Theatre at the time when Bulmer Hobson said, "Damn Yeats! We'll write our own plays!" His main interest was in poetry and in collecting songs, versions of which he published with music arranged by Herbert Hughes. "My Lagan Love" and "The Spanish Lady" are the best known of his songs. He died in Glencree in isolation in 1944.

ETHNA CARBERY (née Anna Johnston) was born in Ballymena in 1866. She married Seumas MacManus the poet and storyteller from Mountcharles, County Donegal, and died in 1902. A lifelong republican, she produced, with Alice Milligan, the magazine, *The Shan-Van-Vocht*. Their poetry and that of her husband was published in a composite volume, *We Sang for Ireland*.

JOHN KEEGAN CASEY was born in Ballinacarrow, Loughan, Co. Westmeath in 1846, the son of a schoolmaster. He worked as a tradesman's clerk but was imprisoned as a Fenian at the age of twenty. He contributed to *The Nation*, using the pen-name "Leo", and is responsible for two very contrasted but equally famous Irish songs, "The Rising of the Moon" and "Maire, My Girl". He died in 1870 as the result of a fall from a cab which was involved in an accident on Carlisle Bridge (now O'Connell Bridge).

ANDREW CHERRY was born in Limerick in 1762, the son of a bookseller. He was an actor and playwright in Ireland before taking over the management of the Theatre Royal, Drury Lane, in 1802. Author of a dozen forgettable and forgotten plays, his fame rests on the stirring concert piece, "The Bay of Biscay" and the often regretted but evergreen "Green Little Shamrock". He died in poverty in Monmouth in 1812.

AUSTIN CLARKE was born in 1896 and lived for most of his boyhood in Mountjoy Street near the Black Church (St Mary's Chapel of Ease) that dominated his childhood imagination and gave him the title of his autobiography. He is a poet of rich colour and vigorous language, deeply stained with Gaelic and attaining to some of the structure and assonance of the early poetry. He died in 1974.

PADRAIC COLUM was born Patrick McCormac Colm in Longford in 1881, the son of the workhouse master. As novelist, playwright and poet he was a considerable figure in the Irish Literary Renaissance. This work has been obscured by the much-anthologised pieces, "An Old Woman of the Roads", "Cradle Song" and "A Drover". His later life was spent in America where he became an authority on folklore. He died in Enfield, Connecticut and was buried in Sutton, County Dublin in 1972.

MAURICE JAMES CRAIG was born in Belfast in 1919 and is known as a poet, an historian (especially of Dublin) and for his commentary upon Irish architecture. He was employed by the English Board of Works as Inspector of Ancient Monuments for eighteen years till 1970 and then returned to live in South Dublin. His "Ballad to a Traditional Refrain" is one of the best pieces written about his native city.

JULIA CRAWFORD was born Louise Matilda Jane Montague, perhaps in County Cavan, in 1799. She was the author of many poems and novels, all of which have passed into obscurity except for the ironclad "Kathleen Mavourneen". She died in 1860.

THOMAS OSBORNE DAVIS, the founder of the Young Ireland Movement, was born in Fermoy, County Cork in 1814. He became a nationalist while studying law at Trinity, an Irish language enthusiast and the educator of O'Connell's peasantry in their Irish heritage. In a series of essays published in *The Nation*, the newspaper he founded with Charles Gavan Duffy, he established the basis of nationhood and in some permanently popular and stirring songs, a means of singing about it. He died of scarlet fever in 1845 and was buried in Mount Jerome.

Sir ARTHUR CONAN DOYLE, the historical novelist, creator of the scientific detective, Sherlock Holmes, and ardent spiritualist, was born in Edinburgh of Irish parents in 1859. He qualified as a doctor but initial poverty drove him to authorship. Sherlock Holmes became an albatross, especially as he hoped to be remembered for his historical romances and early sci-fi novels. He died in 1930.

HELEN SALINA, Lady DUFFERIN the grand-daughter of the wit and dramatist, Richard Brinsley Sheridan, was born in England in 1807. She married the Fourth Marquis of Dufferin and Ava whose lands near Newtownards in County Down still have a tower to her memory. She inherited the Sheridan wit and her grandfather's deftness in turning out a song. She died in 1867.

ROBERT EMMET remains the archetypal Irish patriot-martyr figure because of his youth, his romantic love-affair with Sarah Curran, the quick flare of his rising, his dignified and often quoted speech at his trial and his early death. He was born in 1778 and while at Trinity became one of the leaders of the United Irishmen and a strong influence upon his fellow undergraduate, Tom Moore. He withdrew from Trinity in protest at Fitzgibbon's inquiry and left for the continent. He returned to Ireland in 1802 determined to lead an uprising. When it came (1803) it was riotous rather than revolutionary. He was captured by Major Sirr at Sarah Curran's house at Harold's Cross and executed in Thomas Street, Dublin, on 20 September, 1803.

FRANCIS ARTHUR FAHY one of Ireland's finest song-writers was born in Kinvara, County Galway in 1854. He joined the English civil service in 1873 and after the founding of the Gaelic League in 1893 became president of the London branch. His interest in things Irish never wavered. "The Donovans", "The Ould Plaid Shawl" and "The Queen of Connemara" were for years a staple part of the concert bass's repertoire. He died in Clapham in 1935.

Sir SAMUEL FERGUSON was born in Belfast in 1810 and under the influence of Thomas Davis at Trinity became a nationalist and founder of the Protestant Repeal Association. He withdrew from politics and his legal practice to become Deputy Keeper of Public Records and was knighted for his success in managing this department. His poetry is strongly influenced by his study of Irish mythology but "The Lark in the Clear Air" and "Lament for Thomas Davis" are his best known pieces. While remaining a cultural nationalist, he reverted to Unionism before his death in Howth in 1886.

ROBIN FLOWER was born in Yorkshire in 1881 and devoted his life to Celtic studies. His translation of *An t-Oiléanach* by Thomas O Criomtháin is well known, as is his collection of Blasket essays, *The Western Island*. His book *The Irish Tradition* is one of the most readable accounts of Celtic literature. He died in 1946.

JOHN FRAZER was born in Birr, King's County, in 1804. He became a cabinet-maker and later a contributor of verse to *The Nation* under the pen-name of Jean de Jean. He became editor of the *Trades Advocate* in Dublin. His daughter married Thomas Clark Luby, the Fenian journalist. He died in 1852.

WILLIAM PERCY FRENCH was born in Cloonyquin, County Roscommon in 1854. He was educated, among other places, at Foyle College, Derry and TCD where he took in a leisurely way the degrees of BA (1876) and B Eng (1881). Before becoming an author he was a civil engineer in County Cavan. The change from drains to strains made him the most famous comic-song writer in English with the possible exception of W. S. Gilbert. He was also a skilful instrumentalist and water-colourist. He was editor of the comic paper, *The Jarvey*, and after the death of his first wife, Ettie, in childbirth, he became a theatrical entertainer with a series of partners including Dr Houston Collisson who afterwards became an Anglican priest, and May Laffan. His best songs are well known all over the world but few know that he was the author of the "traditional American" student song "Abdulla Bulbul Ameer". He died in Formby, Lancashire in 1920.

OLIVER ST JOHN GOGARTY, born 1878, was the great Corinthian of his time. Renowned for his poetry and wit, he was a skilful surgeon and aviator and a senator of the Irish Free State. His wit and Grecian temper is best discovered in such books as *As I Was Going Down Sackville Street.* He is the Buck Mulligan of *Ulysses* and probably much better company than his tower companion. He died in 1957.

OLIVER GOLDSMITH was born in 1728 in Pallasmore, County Longford, the son of the local curate. He was educated by a hedge schoolmaster. Rejected for the Church he studied medicine in Edinburgh and in Leyden in Holland. He failed to establish a medical practice in 1756 and became a Grub Street hack in the London of Garrick and Johnson. He became a member of Johnson's club and, in spite of much ephemeral scribbling, had the distinction of writing in *The Vicar of Wakefield* (1776), *The Deserted Village* (1770) and *She Stoops to Conquer* (1778), one each of the most famous novels, poems and plays in English. He died of a fever in London in 1774.

ARTHUR PERCIVAL GRAVES, probably now more famous as the father of the lyric poet and gadfly critic, Robert Graves, had earlier claim to fame as the composer of "Father O'Flynn". He was born in Dublin in 1844, the son of Charles Graves who afterwards became Bishop of Limerick. He graduated from Trinity in 1871 and became, by turns, assistant editor of *Punch,* Home Office Clerk and Inspector of Schools. His book of reminiscences, *To Return to All That* (1930), written when he was eighty-four in riposte to his son's *Goodbye To All That* (1929), is a most entertaining account of one Irish life. He died in Wales in 1931.

GERALD GRIFFIN was born in Limerick in 1803, the ninth son of a brewer. The brewery failed when Gerald was seventeen and his Micawberish father took all of the family except Gerald and his older brother William to Philadelphia. He went to London to earn his living by writing but for several years he was forced to live in penury and severely damaged his health. Eventually he published some stories with help from John Banim and Tom Moore. He returned to Ireland in 1827 and published his famous novel, *The Collegians*, two years later. This formed the basis for Boucicault's most famous play, *The Colleen Bawn*, and Julius Benedict's opera, *The Lily of Killarney*. He became a Christian Brother after an unhappy love affair and died in North Monastery, Cork, in 1840.

JOHN HEWITT was born in Belfast in 1907 and graduated with an MA from Queen's, his thesis written on nineteenth-century Ulster poets. He joined the staff of the Ulster Museum in 1930 and had become Deputy-Director by 1957 when he was appointed Art Director of the Herbert Art Gallery and Museum, Coventry. He returned to Belfast in 1970. He is one of Ulster's leading poets and art-critics. His work has done much to help the northern Protestant to come to some understanding of his past and his position with regard to the other tradition.

NORA HOPPER was born in Exeter in 1871, the daughter of an Army captain. She married W H Chesson in 1901. She wrote the libretto for the Irish opera, *The Sea Swan* in 1903, with help from George Moore. Yeats admired her earlier lyrics but was less keen on her later work. She died in 1906.

JOHN KELLS INGRAM was born near Pettigo in County Donegal in 1823 and educated at Trinity of which he later became Professor of Greek and Vice-Provost. His poem, "The Memory of the Dead" was published anonymously in *The Nation* when he was twenty. Though at no time did he claim to be a nationalist, he never denied authorship. He became President of the Royal Irish Academy in 1892 and died in 1907.

ROBERT DWYER JOYCE was born in Glenosheen, County Limerick in 1830, the younger brother of Patrick Weston Joyce, the historian and educationalist. After some years as a teacher he became a doctor, graduating from Queen's College, Cork, in 1865. While studying medicine he supported himself by writing, contributing poems to *The Nation*. He became Professor of English Literature at Newman's Catholic University and a Member of the Royal Irish Academy. An ardent Nationalist, he left Ireland when the Fenian Day failed to dawn in 1866 and practised medicine in Boston. He returned to Ireland in 1883 and died soon afterwards.

PATRICK KAVANAGH was born in Inishkeen, County Monaghan in 1904 and lived there as farmer, cobbler and poet until his move to Dublin in 1939. He had already made a name for himself as poet and prose-writer with *Ploughman* (1936) and *The Green Fool* (1938). With *The Great Hunger* (1942) he achieved the mixture of fame and abuse that was a feature of the literary life of the period. His largely autobiographical novel, *Tarry Flynn* (1948), confirmed his reputation as a writer, while his prickly and litigious persona gradually mellowed. When he died in 1967 he was held to be one of Ireland's finest poets.

SEAMUS KAVANAGH came from Wexford and was active in 1916 and in the War of Independence. He is known as the author of many popular songs, "Biddy Mulligan", "The Rose of Mooncoin" and "Moonlight in Mayo", which have been sung so often that many have taken them to be traditional and he is rarely credited with the authorship. He died in the nineteen sixties.

PEADAR KEARNEY (sometimes Ó Cearnaigh) was born in Dublin in 1883. He worked in a bicycle shop but his great interest was in theatre and song-writing. He wrote "The Soldiers' Song" in 1907 and lived to see it become the National Anthem of the new state. His other songs include such perennial favourites as "The Tri-coloured Ribbon", "Down by the Glenside" and "Whack Fol The Diddle". Eventually he was taken on as props manager by the Abbey but not before he had finished his time as a house-painter, a vocation he shared with his more famous nephew, Brendan Behan. He left the Abbey in 1916 to live up to the spirit of his songs. He was interned in 1920 and took the Government side in the Civil War. When peace broke out he returned to his trade and died in obscurity in 1942.

WILLIAM KENNEALLY was born in Cloyne, County Cork in 1828 and contributed verse to periodicals under the pseudonym, William of Munster. He was editor of newspapers in Tipperary and Kilkenny where he spent the rest of his life, having served a term as mayor. He died in 1876. His fame now depends upon one song "The Moon behind the Hill" which was published in *The Nation* in 1856.

THOMAS KETTLE was born in Artane, County Dublin, the son of Andrew Kettle, one of Parnell's most able lieutenants in the Land War. He was called to the Irish Bar in 1905 and became first Professor of National Economics at the newly opened UCD. He was elected Nationalist MP for East Tyrone by 16 votes in 1906. He joined the Irish Volunteers in 1913 but decided that Germany was a greater threat to Ireland, the small nation, than England was. He was commissioned in the Dublin Fusiliers and died at the Somme in 1916. A man of great wit and charm, a talented essayist and a potential leader of a modern Ireland, he deprecated the Easter Rising since it did not accord with his version of a "free, united Ireland in a free Europe".

CHARLES JOSEPH KICKHAM was known and loved by earlier generations as the author of *Knocknagow* (1879), surely the most famous of all nineteenth-century Irish books. He was born in Mullinahone, County Tipperary in 1828, the son of a prosperous shopkeeper. He was intended for medicine but an accident with a firearm at the age of thirteen left him deaf and half-blind. He became an active Fenian, one of the editorial staff of *The Irish People* and was sentenced to fourteen years imprisonment. He was less able to withstand the harsh treatment that prison-warders reserved for Fenians than were O'Leary or O'Donovan Rossa. He was released after serving four years almost totally blind and broken in health. He died at his home in Blackrock in 1882.

DENNY LANE was born in Cork in 1818, the only child of Maurice Lane, a distillery owner. He is remembered for two poems, "Carrigdhoun" and "Kate of Araglen" both of which appeared in *The Nation*. He became an engineer and in time the President of the Institute of Gas Engineers of Great Britain. He died in 1899.

WINIFRED LETTS was born in Dublin in 1882, educated at Alexandra College and practised as a masseuse. She contributed several plays to the early Abbey repertoire, notably *The Challenge* (1909) and wrote reminiscences about life in Leinster called *Knockmaroon* (1933). She married W H F Verschoyle. She is mainly remembered today for her lyric "A Soft Day" which was printed in her first collection of poetry, *Songs from Leinster*. She died in 1950.

JOHN LOCKE was born in Callan, County Kilkenny in 1817. He joined the IRB in 1847 and contributed to James Stephens' Fenian journal, *The Irish People*. He had the characteristic Fenian career of journalism, imprisonment, exile and journalism in America. He died in New York in 1889.

SAMUEL LOVER was born in Dublin in 1797, the son of a stockbroker. He trained as a painter and was elected to the Royal Hibernian Academy in 1828. He gave up painting in 1844 when his eyesight began to fail and developed his literary talent which had produced *Legends and Stories of Ireland* (1831) and *Handy Andy* (1842). He devised a theatrical entertainment called *An Irish Evening,* with which he toured and for which he supplied the material. At the age of 59, he received a Civil List pension and died twelve years later at St. Helier, Jersey, in 1868.

EDWARD LYSAGHT was born in County Clare in 1763 and after graduating from Trinity was called to both the English and the Irish Bars. He joined the Irish Volunteers in 1783. He was a strong opponent of the Act of Union. His poems were published in 1811, the year after his death.

DONAGH MACDONAGH was born in Dublin in 1912, the son of Thomas MacDonagh, the 1916 leader. He was called to the Irish Bar in 1936 and became a District Justice in 1941. Well known as poet, wit and broadcaster, his particular contribution to the Irish theatre was a number of verse-plays — "ballad operas without music". *Happy-as-Larry* has tailors, widows and three old ladies from Hades and *Step-in-the-Hollow* is an Irish version of Kleist's *Der Zerbrochene Krug,* in which an amorous judge finds himself in the position of trying a case in which he is the guilty party. He died in 1968.

THOMAS MACDONAGH was born in Cloughjordan, County Tipperary in 1878. He met Pearse in 1908 while he was in Aran to improve his Irish and with him founded St Enda's School in Ranelagh. He joined the English Department of UCD and in 1914 became director of training for the Irish Volunteers. He became a member of the Military Council in 1915 and was one of the chief planners of the Easter Rising, a signatory of the Proclamation of the Republic and commander of the insurgents in Jacobs during the Rising. He was executed on May 3, 1916, along with Pearse and Thomas J. Clarke. He wrote poetry and had been co-founder with Edward Martyn and Joseph Mary Plunkett of the Irish Theatre in Hardwicke Street in 1914.

PATRICK MACGILL was born in Clooney, near Glenties in 1891. He followed the usual path of the Donegal poor, first hiring himself to a Lagan farmer and then heading for Scotland as a "tattie-hoker" and later as a navvy. He was the first to publicise the appalling conditions the Irish migrant workers had to endure and wrote about them in two famous novels, *Children of the Dead End* (1914) and *The Rat Pit* (1915). He had earlier published poetry, including *Songs of a Navvy.* He joined the London Irish in 1914 and was at the front for the war's duration. He died in America in 1963.

GERALD MACNAMARA was the pen-name of Harry Morrow, one of the stalwarts of the Ulster Literary Theatre (see note to p 284).

THOMAS MAGUIRE was an authentic balladeer, singing his own songs at fairs and in the streets. D. J. O'Donoghue, the author of the great comprehensive bibliography of pre-1914 Irish poets notes that he and his wife were charged with obstruction in London in October 1907, that they offered for sale pamphlets in the street. He had, unfortunately, no further information about him.

FRANCIS SYLVESTER MAHONY was born in Cork in 1804, the son of a Blarney wool manufacturer. He studied as a Jesuit and taught in Clongowes. After some minor scandal, he left the Order, but continued his clerical studies at the Irish College in Rome. He was eventually ordained for the Cork diocese and contributed to *Frazer's Magazine* under the name of "Father Prout", the name of an actual Parish Priest. He left Ireland under dispensation and became a journalist, Paris correspondent of *The Daily News.* Mainly a humorous writer, he was also a brilliant linguist and classical scholar. He translated Moore's *Melodies* into Latin and Greek. He called the result *Moore's Plagiarisms,* a joke that Moore did not find funny. He died in 1866 and was buried in the vaults of Shandon Church, Cork, which he had made so famous.

JOHN CLARENCE MANGAN was born plain John Mangan in Fishamble Street, Dublin in 1803, the rather fanciful "Clarence" being added later. He worked as a scrivener's clerk and later at the Ordnance Survey Office. He had been given a free private education by a Father Graham who taught him the modern languages at which he became so proficient. His poverty and addiction to drugs and drink caused a life of almost unrelieved misery. His work in its morbid and hallucinatory aspects much resembles that of Edgar Allan Poe but it is unlikely that the American ever read the Irishman's poems. He died in the cholera epidemic of 1849.

WILLIAM FREDERICK MARSHALL was born in Derebard, County Tyrone in 1888 and brought up in Sixmilecross in the same county, where his father was schoolmaster. He was educated in the Royal School, Dungannon, Queen's College, Galway and Assembly College Belfast where he was ordained a Presbyterian Minister. His main years of ministry were spent in Castlerock, County Derry. He was an authority on Ulster Dialect and was elected a member of the Royal Irish Academy for his work in that sphere. He died in 1959.

WILLIAM MC BURNEY was born in County Down in 1844. He emigrated early to the US and died there in 1892 after a career in journalism. He contributed to *The Nation* under the name of "Carroll Malone".

PATRICK JOSEPH MCCALL was born in Patrick Street, Dublin in 1861. His *Fenian Nights Entertainments* was serialised in *The Shamrock*. These were tales of the Fianna and other Celtic heroes told in appropriate "seanachaí" style. He is remembered today chiefly as the author of many stirring patriotic songs by which he effectively carried on the work of *The Nation* by giving the country songs to sing. He died in 1919.

MICHAEL JOSEPH MCCANN was born in Galway in 1824 and joined the staff of St Jarlath's, Tuam, a protege of Archbishop MacHale. He later went to London and became a journalist, for a time the editor of a short-lived periodical, *The Harp*. He died in London in 1883.

THOMAS D'ARCY MCGEE was born in Carlingford, County Louth in 1825. He emigrated to Boston when he was seventeen and became editor of *The Boston Eagle* in 1846. He was a vigorous orator and a committed nationalist and he was inevitably attracted to the Young Ireland Movement. He contributed much to *The Nation* of which he became London editor. After Smith O'Brien's minor rising of 1848, he ceased to support armed revolution and became instead a constitutional reformer. He returned to Boston and in 1858 emigrated to Canada where he had an active career in politics. He denounced a projected invasion of Canada by American Fenians and was assassinated in 1868 presumably at the behest of former colleagues who had viewed his behaviour over the previous twenty years as betrayal.

KUNO MEYER was born in Hamburg in 1859 and while lecturing in German in Liverpool became interested in Celtic Languages. He founded the Summer School of Irish Learning in 1903 and became editor of its journal, *Eriú*, in 1904. As such he was one of the key figures in the modern revival of Irish. He became Professor of Celtic in Berlin in 1911 and died in Leipzig in 1919. He was made a freeman of Dublin in 1911 and of Cork in 1912.

JAMES LYNAM MOLLOY was born in Cornelare, King's County, in 1837, graduated from Newman's University and was later called to the English Bar. He practised hardly at all but made a fine career both as composer and librettist. His first success was "Beer, Beer, Beautiful Beer" and he wrote the music for the world famous "Love's Old Sweet Song". His Irish fame rests on "The Kerry Dance" and "Bantry Bay". He died in 1907.

THOMAS FRANCIS MULLAN was born near Ardmore, Co. Derry in 1860. He taught in Derry and later became headmaster of Faughanvale PES. He collaborated with a Derry music teacher, Edward Conaghan, in the writing of a *'98 Cantata* devised to commemorate the centenary of the Rising. He died in 1937.

THOMAS MOORE was born in Dublin in 1799, the son of a Kerry father and a Wexford mother, Anastasia Codd. She was the major influence in his life, found the money to send him to Trinity and encouraged him to go to London to study law in the Middle Temple. He was friendly with Emmet and other United Irishmen and though he took no part in their activities, maintained a strong, if constitutionalist, nationalist stance all his life. He was a gifted light poet and in his time much more highly regarded than his friend Byron whose memoirs he burnt. The oriental verse-romance *Lalla Rookh* made a lot of money for him, "the crame of the copyright", as he called it but he instinctively valued the *Irish Melodies* as his more lasting contribution to literature. It was also his greatest service, for in spite of much modern criticism, he undoubtedly dignified the name of Ireland and still remains her greatest songster. He died after a period of premature senility in his Wiltshire cottage and was buried at Bromham in 1852.

WILLIAM MULCHINOCK was born near Tralee, County Kerry, in 1820. Although a Protestant, he was a supporter of Daniel O'Connell and had to flee the country after an affray for which he was held responsible. He returned to Ireland in 1849 and died in 1864. His fame is linked with that of his famous song "The Rose of Tralee" which he wrote for a lost sweetheart.

DELIA MURPHY was born in Galway, the daughter of a professor at UCG. She was a tremendously popular entertainer in the forties, as a singer of such songs as "Moonlight in Mayo" and "The Moonshiner." Her husband, T. H. Kiernan was Irish Ambassador to Rome during the War.

FLANN O'BRIEN was one of the *personae* (the term pen-name is inadequate) of the many-sided literary genius who was born Brian O'Nolan in Strabane, County Tyrone, in 1912. Well known as an *Irish Times* columnist with *Cruiskeen Lawn*, as a novelist and playwright and as a great heavy-lidded observer of the mad Irish, his early death in 1966 robbed the country of one of its wits and salutary gad-flies.

JOHN A O'BRIEN was the working name of a Father Hartigan who was born of Irish parents in Yass, New South Wales. He was Parish Priest of Narrandera and with his book *Around the Boree Log* became known as "the poet laureate of the Irish settlers in Australia."

JOHN O'KEEFE was born in Dublin in 1747 and trained as a painter. He went on the stage and later became very famous in his time as the author of many plays. He went blind in 1790 but with his daughter's help continued to write. He died in 1833. His play *Wild Oats* was successfully revived by the Royal Shakespeare Company in 1976.

MARY DAVENPORT O'NEILL was born in Loughrea, County Galway in 1893. She was educated at the National College of Art and married the historical novelist, Joseph O'Neill. She wrote several verse plays and some poetry but was chiefly famous for her Dublin literary salon. She died in 1967.

MOIRA O'NEILL was the literary name of Agnes Skrine, née Higginson. She wrote a collection of dialect poems, *Songs of the Glens of Antrim,* which were very popular since their publication in 1907. Her daughter, Molly Keane, is well known as a novelist, both under her own name and as M. J. Farrell.

ARTHUR WILLIAM EDGAR O'SHAUGHNESSY was born in London of Irish parents in 1844. He worked as a transcriber in the British Museum and afterwards in the National History Department when it was transferred to South Kensington. He died in 1881, having had a brief spell of fame as a rather world-weary poet.

JOHNNY PATTERSON was born in Feakle, County Clare in 1840. He was a well-known circus clown and in characteristic Irish fashion interspersed his clowning with sentimental songs, most of which he wrote himself. He was killed in Tralee in 1889 after a political meeting.

PATRICK HENRY PEARSE was born in Dublin in 1879 the son of an Irish mother and an English father. He was educated at the CBS in Westland Row and at the Royal University. He became a barrister but rarely practised. His ideal of a free and Gaelic Ireland led to the founding of a school, St Enda's, dedicated to his own carefully thought-out ideas of education. He joined the IRB in America and became the first President of the Provisional Irish Republic which was promulgated on the steps of the GPO, Dublin on Easter Monday, 1916. He and his brother Willie were executed in Kilmainham on May 3, 1916.

ANTHONY RAFTERY, alias Antoine O'Reachtabhra, was born about 1784 in County Mayo. He went blind from small-pox in his youth and became a travelling poet and fiddler mainly in East Galway. His work was collected by Douglas Hyde. He died in 1835.

WILLIAM ROONEY was born in Dublin in 1872 and was closely associated with Arthur Griffith in the literary beginnings of Sinn Féin. He was a keen worker for the revival of Irish and broke his health in his labours. He died in 1901.

GEORGE WILLIAM RUSSELL (self-renamed AE from the word "aeon" which had mystic significance for him) was born in Lurgan, County Armagh in 1867, so that John B. Yeats's description "A saint but born in Portadown" was about five miles out. He became interested in the Cooperative Movement and was Sir Horace Plunkett's best lieutenant in the IAOS. His journal, the *Irish Statesman* was a handy outlet for publication of the works of many apprentice Irish writers. He was a colleague and wary friend of Yeats, and rather more generous to the young than he. A poet and atmospheric painter, his limited private life was taken up with mysticism. He died in 1935.

ELIZABETH SHANE was born Gertrude Hind, somewhere in Ulster and sometime towards the end of the last century. She was the daughter of a clergyman who was sometime incumbent of Bunbeg, County Donegal. She published several volumes of verse about West Donegal, and in particular the parishes of Gweedore and the Rosses. In spite of such a dearth of information about her, she has had a much greater impact than many a more famous writer with her recitation "Wee Hughie" which was known to generations of Northern schoolchildren.

CHARLES DAWSON SHANLY was born in Dublin in 1811 and educated at Trinity. He followed a career taken by many Irishmen of that century, politics followed by emigration followed by a successful career in journalism. He died in Florida in 1875.

RICHARD BRINSLEY SHERIDAN was born in Dublin in 1751 but made his career as playwright, theatre-manager and politician in England. He was a brilliant orator and wit in an age when these qualities were appreciated and it fell to him as it has done regularly to the Irish since to supply the English stage with classical comedy. His *School for Scandal* and *The Rivals* have never dropped out of the repertoire. He died in poverty because of drink and poor financial management in 1816.

RICHARD STANIHURST was born in Dublin in 1547 and educated at Oxford and Lincoln's Inn. His tutor was Edward Campion who was executed by Elizabeth I. He wrote verse and Latin history and became a priest after his wife's death. He died in 1618.

TIMOTHY DANIEL SULLIVAN was born in Bantry, County Cork in 1827. He became a journalist and later co-editor with his brother Alexander Martin of *The Nation*, which they acquired when Charles Gavan Duffy left for Australia. He was MP for Westmeath, Dublin and Donegal between 1880 and 1890. He edited the great nineteenth-century staple of patriotic bookshelves, *Speeches from the Dock*, but as his politics became cooler began to regret his song for the Manchester Martyrs, "God Save Ireland". He died in 1914.

JONATHAN SWIFT was born in Dublin in 1667 and after a brilliant career foundered in obscurity as Dean of St Patrick's Cathedral, due to the ascendancy of the Whigs and the personal animus of Queen Anne. He was the greatest satirist of his age, indeed of any age in modern times. His love affairs with Hester Johnson and Esther Vanhomrigh, strangely pursued and probably not consummated, have fascinated later ages. He suffered from the undiagnosed Meuniere's Syndrome and died after three years of torpor in 1745.

JOHN MILLINGTON SYNGE was born at Rathfarnham, County Dublin, in 1871. He graduated from Trinity after intermittent attendance and with a qualification in Irish. He travelled in France and Germany intending a career in music. Yeats claimed to have sent him to the Aran Islands and indeed there he discovered his real career as a latter-day Jacobean comedian. His are the only certain works of genius of the Abbey theatre. He died of lymphatic cancer in 1909.

NAHUM TATE was born in Dublin in 1652. After graduation he moved to England and quickly became part of the literary scene. He was a friend of Dryden and like him an "improver" of Shakespeare. His version of *King Lear* has a happy ending with Edgar marrying Cordelia and it was the preferred version until 1850 when the original text was restored. He became Poet Laureate in 1692 and was not the worst of the creatures who accepted that miserable post. He died in 1715.

CHARLOTTE ELIZABETH TONNA was born in Norwich in 1790, the daughter of the Rev. Michael Browne. She lived in Kilkenny and wrote many tracts of an evangelical nature for the Dublin Tracts Society. Like her younger contemporary, C.F.A., she was drawn to write verse about the Seige of Derry, especially "No Surrender" and "The Maiden City". She died in Kilkenny in 1846.

KATHARINE TYNAN was born in Dublin in 1861 and played a minor but not insignificant part in the Irish Literary Renaissance. Her father's house in Clondalkin was a meeting-place for the young literary men of the time. It was probably there that Yeats met Hyde for the first time. She married H. A. Hinkson in 1883 and lived with him in County Mayo where he was RM until his death in 1919. She wrote much poetry and many novels but only a few of her song-lyrics have survived. She died in 1931.

HELEN WADDELL was born in Tokyo in 1889 but spent much of her life in Belfast. She was a distinguished Latin scholar, an authority on the medieval church. Her version of the Heloise and Abelard story is the most attractive. Her brother, Sam, was the "Rutherford Mayne" of the Ulster Literary Theatre, the author of *The Drone*, the best of the early Ulster plays. She died in 1965.

JOHN FRANCIS WALLER was born in Limerick in 1809 and followed a well-trod path of graduation from Trinity, a term or two at the Irish Bar and then a career in journalism. He succeeded Charles Lever as editor of the *Dublin University Magazine*. Later he edited and wrote many entries of *The Imperial Dictionary of Universal Biography* (1857-1863). He is remembered as the author of some very popular songs, notably, "Cushla Ma Chree" and "The Spinning Wheel". He died in 1894.

THOMAS 1st Marquis WHARTON was born in 1648 and became an active supporter of William III against James II. In reward he was made Lord-Lieutenant of Ireland in 1702. He was made marquis in the year of his death, 1714.

RICHARD D'ALTON WILLIAMS was born in Dublin in 1822, the illegitimate son of Count D'Alton. He studied medicine and finally became a doctor but not before he had begun to contribute much verse to *The Nation* under the name "Shamrock". He was arrested in 1848 for "treason-felony" and successfully defended by Sir Samuel Ferguson. He emigrated to America in 1851 and there had a mixed career as academic and doctor. He died of the same disease that forms the background to his most famous poem, "The Dying Girl", in 1862.

WILLIAM GORMAN WILLIS was born in Kilkenny in 1828, the cousin of both Edith Somerville and Violet Martin of "The Irish RM" fame. He failed to graduate from Trinity and spent his young manhood "daisy-picking". He became a painter and later a writer. He died in 1891.

FLORENCE M. WILSON was born in Warrenpoint sometime towards the end of the last century and died in Bangor in 1947. She is remembered as the composer of the great recitation "The Man from God-Knows-Where."

CHARLES WOLFE was born in Blackhall, County Kildare in 1791. Educated at Trinity, he refused the offer of a fellowship because he did not relish the prospect of celibacy. He became a curate in 1817 and wrote his famous ode "On the Burial of Sir John Moore" that same year. It was published anonymously in the *Newry Telegraph*. He died of tuberculosis in the Cove of Cork in 1823 after being rejected by the lady he wished to marry. He was related to Wolfe Tone and to the General Wolfe who died capturing Quebec in 1759.

ZOZIMUS was the "pen-name" of Michael Moran, the glee-man, who was one of the characters of Dublin in the early part of the last century. He was born in Faddle Alley, off Clanbrassil Street in 1794 and, although blind from near birth and having really a poor ear for music, nevertheless made a living as a street entertainer. His ballads such as "St Patrick was a Gentleman" are still known. He died at Easter time in 1846.

Index of Titles

A Christmas Childhood   192
All Things Bright and Beautiful   317
A Modest Proposal   235
A Nation Once Again   101
A Pint of Plain is Your Only Man   282
Aqua Vitae   233
A Soft Day   170
At Oranmore   134

Ballad to a Traditional Refrain   283
Bantry Bay   186
Biddy Mulligan: the Pride of the Coombe   115
Bold Phelim Brady, Bard of Armagh   39
Bold Robert Emmet   73
Boolavogue   67
By the Short Cut to the Rosses   327

Cailín Deas Crúite na mBó   199
Carrigdhoun   212
Cockles and Mussels   117
Columcille the Scribe   313
Come Back, Paddy Reilly   342
Coortin' in the Kitchen   250
Corrymeela   348
County Mayo   113

Danny   153
Dark Rosaleen   50
Dawn on the Irish Coast   124
Dicey Reilly   118
Dolly's Brae   41
Dublin Made Me   140

Easter 1916: Proclamation of the Irish Republic   84

Father O'Flynn   268
Four Ducks on a Pond   148

Galway   133
God Save Ireland   103
Going Home   131
Golden Stockings   224
Gortnamona   221

I am Ireland   107
I am Raftery   91
I Don't Mind If I do   254
If I was a Blackbird   227
If I was a Lady   187
I Know my Love   204
I'll Sing Thee Songs of Araby   215
I'll Tell My Ma   137
Ireland Delineated   90
I Saw from the Beach   179
I Shall Not Go To Heaven   190

John-John   222
Johnny I Hardly Knew Ye   237

Kathleen Mavourneen   205
Kitty of Coleraine   203

Lament of the Irish Maiden   212
Last Words   30
Let Him Go, Let Him Tarry   256
Let the Toast Pass   242
Lillibuléro   21

Maire, My Girl   218
Marching Song of Fiach MacHugh   69
Mary from Dungloe   350
Me an' me Da   171

My Aunt Jane   191
My Lagan Love   225
My Mary of the Curling Hair   207

O Bay of Dublin   335
O'Donnell Abu   56
Oh! The Praties They are Small Over Here   43
Off to Philadelphia   340
Old Skibbereen   44
On Behalf of Some Irishmen Not Followers of Tradition 105
On the Banks of My Own Lovely Lee   129

Panegyric at the Graveside of O'Donovan Rossa   77
Pangur Bán   311
Phil the Fluther's Ball   270
Protestant Boys   92

Renunciation   108
Riders to the Sea   155
Rody McCorley   71

St. Patrick's Breastplate   309
Shancoduff   176
Sheep and Lambs   320
She Is Far From the land   96
She Moved Through the Fair   226
Shlathery's Mounted Fut   272
Silent O Moyle   316
Sir Boyle Roche   244
Slievenamon   214
Solemn League and Covenant   86
Song from the Backwoods   336
Song for July 12th, 1843   99
Stanzas on Women   240

The Agricultural Irish Girl   249
The Ballad of Henry Joy   37

The Ballad of William Bloat   280
The Battle of the Boyne   24
The Bells of Shandon   122
The Boys of Wexford   60
The Burial of Sir John Moore   35
The Celts   58
The Croppy Boy   62
The Cruiskeen Lawn   52
The Donovans   151
The Dying Girl   181
The Emigrant's Letter   346
The Enniskillen Dragoon   201
The Fairies   184
The Finding of Moses   247
The Friar of Orders Gray   241
The Garden Where the Praties Grow   216
The Gartan Mother's Lullaby   189
The Green Little Shamrock   94
The Irish Colonel   66
The Irish Dancer   89
The Irish Emigrant   333
The Lark in the Clear Air   211
The Last Rose of Summer   180
The Liberator and Biddy Moriarty   275
The Low-Backed Car   145
The Maid of the Sweet Brown Knowe   258
The Maiden City   33
The Man from God-Knows-Where   80
The Meeting of the Waters   114
The Memory of the Dead   54
The Men of the West   75
The Minstrel Boy   95
The Moon Behind the Hill   331
The Mountains of Mourne   344
The Next Market Day   147
The Old Bog Road   338
The Old Orange Flute   260

The Orange Lily-o	97
The Ould Lammas Fair	136
The Planter's Daughter	228
The Pretty Milkmaid	199
There's Whiskey in the Jar	262
The Rising of the Moon	64
The Rose of Aranmore	206
The Rose of Mooncoin	229
The Rose of Tralee	213
The Sash my Father Wore	98
The Shan Van Vocht	46
The Spanish Lady	127
The Spinning Wheel	209
The Stone Outside Dan Murphy's Door	149
The Trimmin's on the Rosary	322
The Wayfarer	169
The Wearing of the Green	29
The West's Asleep	52
The Women are Worse than the Men	266
Thompson in Tir-na-nOg	284
Three Lovely Lasses in Bannion	174
Tim Finnegan's Wake	264
To my daughter Betty, the Gift of God	326
Tone is Coming Back Again	48
Trottin' to the Fair	219
Ulster Names	138
Waxies Dargle	120
"We are the music-makers"	319
Wee Hughie	195
Whack Fol the Diddle	278
While Shepherds Watched their Flocks by Night	314